The Wreck

· · · · · · · · · · · · · · ·

The Wreck was originally
published in French as *L'Epave*
in 2005 by Editions Madrépores.
This English edition was first
published in 2011 by little island press.

Published by little island press,
P. O. Box 78-397, Grey Lynn,
Auckland 1245, New Zealand
www.littleisland.co.nz

201212301117

ISBN 978-1-877484-16-2

Editing: Pepperleaf Publishing

This book was published with the assistance
of the French Government

The Wreck

Déwé Gorodé

Translated and with a critical introduction by
Deborah Walker-Morrison and Raylene Ramsay

little island press

Introduction

L'Epave [*The Wreck*] was first published in 2005[1] in New Caledonia, a French overseas country *sui generis*, presently negotiating new pathways toward forms of greater autonomy, "common destiny", or independence. The 1998 *Accords de Nouméa* [Noumea Agreement] and the subsequent progressive socio-political "rebalancing" and transfer of powers from France have opened up possibilities for an emancipatory future, but equally for significant conflict. From 2018, the question of independence will be put to popular ballot in a series of referenda.

This first Kanak novel thus emerges against the background of turbulent socio-political contexts in a country in political transition, where the citizens of Kanak (44%), European (38%) and other origins are considering their future together. It is also of significance that two of the three Provinces created by the Noumea Agreements are controlled by Kanak, still largely living in *tribus*, or "customary lands", according to customary structures.

The Wreck is also the first published novel of Déwé Gorodé, poet, writer, independence activist, and for a number of years, Vice-President of the post Noumea Agreement, "Collegial" New

Caledonian government. Retrieved in 2004 from one of many notebooks of creative writing, handwritten in French and hidden away in a cardboard box, this somewhat sulphurous, and fiercely critical, insider text took on a public life in Noumea in 2005, put into print by the small local New Caledonian press, Madrépores. Despite the scandal and incomprehension created by its sexual thematics, the book went into a second edition and in 2010, the Auckland based, New Zealand publisher, Little Island Press, accepted the challenge to make this curious novel from the French-speaking Pacific available in English translation.

Déwé Gorodé was born on June 1ˢᵗ 1949, in the *tribu de l'Embouchure*, near Ponérihouen, in the Paicî language area of the East Coast of New Caledonia.[2] "I started to love writing at a very young age", she remembers. No doubt because she already loved listening to stories, whether from her own land or from those far away. "My father used to tell us stories in Paicî: fairytales like *Tom Thumb* and stories from Victor Hugo's *Les Miserables*. My big sisters would bring home book prizes, reading books, I devoured them all." Later, the bookworm would become a storyteller herself.

Among the first Kanak to study at university level in France, her career as a writer really began during the years spent as an undergraduate literature student at Montpellier University (1969–1973). It was here that she began writing poetry, discovered the African writers of the Negritude movement (Senghor, Césaire, Damas), the romantics, and Marx.... Her time spent in France thus marks the twin discovery of writing and politics. When she returned home, she joined a number of Kanak protest groups and in May 1976, she was a founding member of the Palika pro-independence party. As the party's foreign affairs spokesperson, she travelled the world with other members of the movement, advocating for Kanak Independence across the Pacific, speaking in Australia, Algeria, Canada, Mexico and at the UN.

On completing her Bachelor's degree in French literature, she entered the teaching profession in 1974, teaching French, Paicî , and later Pacific literature, in a number of schools around the Island. In 1985, she took part in the experimental indigenous schools, *Ecoles populaires kanak*, set up following the political Troubles that rocked the country in 1984.

Her commitment to political protest and to the independence movement led to her being imprisoned in Nouméa's Camp-Est on two occasions, in 1974 and 1977. It was here that she wrote part of her first anthology of poetry, *Sous les cendres des conques / Under the Ashes of the Conch Shells*, published in 1984, and which demonstrates her determination to express the Kanak quest for self-determination and her deep attachment to her cultural roots. In this work she attempted a "poetic interpretation of History". For many long years, however, political struggle was to take precedence over writing. "This is perhaps also why I took such a long time to have my work published", she explains.

Déwé Gorodé has to date published three volumes of poems, two volumes of short stories, including a novella[3] and a play. The latter, *Kanaké 2000*, was staged in 1999, by Pierre Gope, an indigenous playwright from the Loyalty Island of Maré. Critic and conscience of her society, Gorodé's writing, first and foremost, foregrounds Kanak values and traditions, and in particular, women's experience. Her *parti-pris* of indigeneity seeks to write outside, rather than simply "back to", the European world and to capitalism. Gorodé's characters are most often self-effacing but strong women, living in the service of the extended family and transmitting ancestral knowledge and Kanak ways of being in the world.

Like other of her contemporaries, such as the Kanak artist Micheline Néporon, whose powerful re-presentation of the colonial photograph of "Betty" in a mission dress portrays a dignified but already hybrid figure of silent despair, Gorodé's work denounces the destruction wrought by colonization and modernization on a predominantly oral society regulated for more than half a century by the colonial French Native Code.[4] Her texts articulate the losses involved in assimilation to French norms by a very different culture only just emerging from its long exclusion from the economic and political mainstream.

> **Writing**
> writing
> an island
> a land
> where beings once were
> where beings were without being
> speechless
> lifeless
> visionless
> voiceless
> beneath the heavy cloak
> of silence
> clear felled
> by the single way of thinking...[5]

The space where Gorodé's personal story begins is within the *tribu* (the term refers to both the people of the clan and its territories, now designated by the French Administration as "customary lands"), beside the sea at Ponérihouen (Pwârâiriwâ) on the East Coast of the Grande-Terre [Main Island] – named, explains Gorodé, for its relation to the neighbouring archipelago of the Loyalty Islands. The wider historical contexts are the annexation of the Grande-Terre by France in 1853, the establishment of a penal colony and allocation of the greater part of the land to settlers of European origin, and the resettlement of the excluded Kanak groups together in "reserves". The time of her narrative, then, is twofold: The time of residual memory of traditional life, and the history of colonization.

"As soon as a *popwaalé* –[white person] turned up – most of the time a farmer or a gendarme – all the women would run away and hide in the coffee bushes and we kids would go running away behind them." The *popwaalé,* as Gorodé observes, in this oral account of her childhood, only saw and talked with the men.[6] Many of Gorodé's early poems raise the both personal and political question of the status of women, not in a consistently feminist frame in the Western sense – which Gorodé would partly disavow – but alongside the issues of the legacy of colonization, poverty, social injustice, the degradation of tradition and sexual abuse.

With Back Bowed
Day breaks
on the roof of the thatch house
where lies sleeping between her parents
the child I once was
...
where the ruling masters
are liars
and impostors
fraudsters
and forgers
of our customs
...
children to feed
going to school
through the mangrove
while the hurrying father
slides a groping hand
towards the daughter's thigh
...
on the floor of the shanty
knocked out with booze and dope
to forget her
prostitute state of
paternal rape

Day breaks
on the roof of a thatch house
where lies sleeping between her parents
the child I once was.[7]

The Wreck is making its appearance as customary societies within
the French Republic attempt to adapt in order to implement the
recently mandated law on political 'parity' and as debate rages in New
Caledonia on issues such as the composition of, and procedures of
election to, the all-male Customary Senate. Gorodé has made very
public stands on women's rights to representation, and this political
position is evident in her fictional writing despite her recognition
of the very particular position of Kanak women within a patriarchal
customary society to which they nonetheless maintain their first
allegiance.

In her 1996 novella, *Utê Mûrûnû, petite fleur de cocotier* – which
recounts the lives of five generations of women, all named Uté
Mûrûnû (little coconut flower), war-booty, victims of arranged
marriage, of abandonment, or of the loss of sons and husbands in
war and all looking for legitimately female ways of getting around
the insurmountable 'rock' of male-dominated tradition – Gorodé
suddenly addresses her reader in a rhetorical prose of radical protest
that is also redolent of traditional (male) speech-making.

> Bearers of seed, we were bound and gagged by prohibitions,
> branded with taboos that were like rocks blocking the paths of life
> [...] Ädi, black pearls of customary marriage, we were exchanged
> like pieces of Lapita pottery to seal an alliance, in between two
> wars. Matrimonial pathways linking the clans, we survived as best
> we could a childhood and an entry into adolescence that was too
> often violated by the lecherous desires of senior men. Prestige,
> virility, war – male concepts for the Great House of men, built
> on the broad backs of women! Sharing, solidarity, humility, the

word of women, conceived, nourished, and carried in our entrails of beaten wives.[8]

Like Grace Mera Molisa in Vanuatu, whose post-independence poems celebrating the *Black Stone* of Melanesian values she translated,[9] a militant Gorodé voices protest at what both women writers present as the 'double colonization' of women. This is the didactic voice heard again in *The Wreck* – at the funeral of (Da)Lila, the murdered young street-woman story-teller who, in retelling the stories of oral tradition, nonetheless makes their often devious underlying sexual messages explicit. Like most of the female characters, Lila is also an incest survivor and a victim of the constantly metamorphosing character, Old Tom. In this text, however, the denunciation of male violence and domination takes the form of a generalized and evidently 'feminist' cry against women's continued commodification in a global market economy: Gorodé's anti-capitalist ideological positioning also enables her to attenuate the attack on her own society.

> The icy peacefulness of death has fixed Lila's features in a serenity outside of the time of the living.... Its violations and its violence. Its unpunished crimes. Children violated, women victims of violence. Unpunished crimes perpetrated by carpet salesmen, arms' dealers and dream merchants who use and abuse the female body like some fine filly or some brood mare up for sale in classifieds, commercials and/or on bill boards on every street corner... Jack the Ripper isn't dead. Even in a little Pacific town, on the other side of the world from the back streets of Mister Hyde's Soho.

Moving edgily between a critique of the violence of colonization, a protest against the global exploitation of women's bodies, and an uncompromising gaze at the underside of Custom, Gorodé's novel attempts to mitigate the impact of its revelations by showing that its criticism of violence against women is both anchored in particular historical and social contexts and resonates beyond Kanak society. In fact, perplexing many of her readers, Gorodé's fiction leaves the question of the origins of violence against women open, partially undecideable.

The Wreck nonetheless picks up and re-weaves, in bold and eye-catching patterns, the threads of what has become a central *topos* in emerging literatures right across the Pacific. So-called 'domestic' or 'conjugal' violence and the spectres of sexual abuse of children, for example, have recently mobilized the Australian government to sponsor a (fiercely contested) program of military and medical 'intervention' in the small aboriginal towns of that country's Northern Territory.

In New Caledonia, the field work of Christine Salomon and Christine Hamelin points to the excesses of a warrior culture in which masculinity and sexual violence or domination are closely connected. The two social scientists argue for the existence of a general male social-isation towards sexual predation, noting, for example, that in times past, certain clubs were given the form of the male sexual organ also often considered a weapon, "his war" in a Paicî language expression. Their claims are supported by a 2003 survey which found that 12.5% of kanak women interviewed, without any significant variation between generations, had experienced forced first sexual intercourse. [10]

However, despite Kanak women's need to speak out, to counter the violence of both outsider or insider domination and rewrite the male-dominated myths that surround them, identification of, engagement with, and resistance to sexual violence in Gorodé's insider novel presents the question in terms of sexual possession and as more complex, more multi-layered in its effects than the sociological texts can know. Moreover, despite the need to "unpick the stitches" from sewn up mouths, certain aspects of women's public silence can also constitute a form of resistance. In Gorodé, the voices of the earth, those heard by Utê Mûrûnû, for example, are identified with a core of local and shared women's values of silence, discretion, self-effacement and sharing. These are recovered through feminized images of roots stretching down into the earth — "nurturing belly/

gentle milk breast mother/this earth, this land/ this mossy softness".[11] Gorodé's solutions to violence in fact remain paradoxically double, even dissonant, engaging both with giving value to feminine Kanak heritage and ways of being and also with the attractions of deviance and male sexual domination.

It has been widely observed in postcolonial literature that given that brutal treatment of women has been a stereotype of "savage mascu-linity" "regularly activated in colonial representations for pragmatic imperial purposes",[12] disclosure and criticism of domestic violence in indigenous societies from the inside is inevitably fraught. Nor can the shame, rage, or emotional turmoil that mark coerced bodies be dissociated from contexts of unequal socio-economic power. The reactions of indigenous activists and writers also include imperatives of solidarity with a partner or group of origin as well as the wider question of the possibility of return to the roots of one's tradition.

In Alan Duff's New Zealand Maori novel, *Once Were Warriors*,[13] for example, Beth initially accepts being beaten by Jake, himself disempowered in a marginalized and violent urban culture, in an attempt to preserve the family unit and keep a sexual partner with whom she shares a largely Māori social world. Despite their rejection of physical dominance or punishment as a way of relating or sorting out authority, novels by Patricia Grace, Witi Ihimaera, Keri Hulme (New Zealand), Albert Wendt, Sia Figiel (Samoa), and Titaua Peu (Tahiti) all recognize and engage with the complexity and, in some cases, the 'perversity' of Pacific women's (and children's) situations in the face of male violence.

When her mother took her to Nouméa for the first time, at the age of eight, Déwé asked her about the identity of the statue of Colonel Gally Passebosc, killed putting down the 1878 Kanak revolt. Her mother, the daughter remembers, told her that it was a monument to Ataï, the Kanak chief who had led the rebellion. And if Déwé herself writes fiction to rehabilitate the place of the Kanak in their own history, as she puts it, it is also because "the political discourse that I myself used, colonisers — colonised, does not account for the perversity and ambiguity of the real relationship between the colonisers and the colonised in the past and in the present".[14] This applies similarly to "double colonisation". Daughter of her resistant (and perverse) mother, Déwé's public mentors were, however, necessarily her grandfathers, pastors who worked as informants for the European ethnographer-pastor, Maurice Leenhardt, men, who alone could officially be orators, delegated with the authority to speak before and on behalf of the group. And the knowledge embedded in their stories, has the status of a very particular (non-European) history, geography, and science, including the knowledge of a certain "perversity" within gender relations. Waia Gorodé, Déwé's father was himself the author of an eclectic as yet unpublished text, *Mon école du silence* [My School of Silence], in which, he challenges the missionary teaching of the sinfulness of the sexual body.

The notion of perversity is of course not itself sufficient to explain the "difference" in these texts. Literatures commonly designated as emerging or indigenous are not so much "new literatures" as bodies of fiction recognized as bringing a new vision of the world (and, as a corollary, new ways of writing). They take their place less within, than alongside, the mainstream European literary traditions with which they are in complex and often unequal dialogue. In the attempt to account for the movements to-and-fro between tradition and modernity, between indigenous and Western societies, and to address both sets of readership, indigenous Pacific writing is more often than not, hybrid, didactic, even confrontational. This creates problems for editors and readers alike: the story/history of the publication of this novel in translation has itself been fraught. However, much to their credit, the present editors have accepted to publish *The Wreck* without cuts and modifications of the original text.

Gorodé may partially succeed in putting a very receivable local Kanak vision, a sense of both community and enchantment back into a Cartesian world. But the enchantment of this world also has a darker and less comprehensible side. *The Wreck* courageously stages the question of incestuous violence against very young women and its longer-term effects in the form of a very material sexual possession. Moreover, Gorodé's apparently postcolonial novel sets the staging and concealment of personal experiences of sexuality and love (somewhat in the tradition of Laclos' *Dangerous Liaisons*) and the construction of her intrigue alongside a series of overtly didactic passages. Gorodé's underlining the need for young people to protect themselves against venereal disease and AIDS clearly derives from the experience of this former Minister for Youth and Recreation; her insistence on the false paradises of alcohol and drugs or consumerism and the socio-political are cultural messages that for many Pacific writers, constitute the custodial responsibilities of the indigenous. And if her novel produces at least a partial answer to the questions of possession, these are spoken in the warp and weft of multiple and sometimes competing voices which may or may not be those of a metamorphosing author-protagonist, who, much like her central trickster-character Old Tom, might well observe, "Now you see me and now you don't".

"The soul is gone from this word emptied thrown out trashed".[15] In some respects, *The Wreck* follows on from Gorodé's earlier critique of a Custom that is as much a product of colonial history and of the corrupting influences of modernity as of an originary Tradition. Since her earliest book of poems, *Sous les cendres des conques* [*Under the Ashes of the Conch Shells*], or her collection of aphorisms in *Par les temps qui courent* [*Signs of the Times*], the writer has been denouncing the problems that unequal power within Custom creates for sexual relations, as in her poem, 'Questions':

Anxious terror of beatings
blows sometimes fatal
Cooking pots thrown around under the coffee bushes
... at the meeting, in front of everyone
he will speak of oppression,
of freedom,
... whose freedom, whose oppression, who by, who with, who for ?[16]

The weighting in her work has shifted, however, from stories that associated sorcery, jealousy, and the disintegration of a traditional marriage with a fiancé from the scraped and wounded lands of the industrial mines ("The Kanak Apple Season"), to an oscillation in *The Wreck* between an orator who comes from "elsewhere" and speaks French, and an Old Tom, initiated by a pagan and polygamous grandfather and identified as much with the cannibal male ancestors as with the primal universal figure of the Ogre.

The central story among the many intertwined narratives in *The Wreck* is that of a quest, the account of young Léna's (as indeed the narrator's and the reader's) journey to the awareness of a repressed childhood trauma. It is something, says Léna, like the excitement of a detective sensing he's about to uncover the clue that will open the gates of truth. "Naked, cruel, indecent – whatever. I must have the truth. And I will track it down until it blows up in my face." The text traces the power of this repressed experience of the discovery of sexuality, of the loss of childhood innocence in a situation of being abusively controlled, firstly as it casts a shadow over Léna's discovery of love with young Tom and later, as it pushes her back, unbeknownst to herself, into the arms of her aggressor, the orator, becoming for a time, his sexual "slave". When Léna finally comes to remember the experience of being raped by the orator as a child on the black rock shaped like the prow of the ancestral canoe, like generations of young women before her, as Old Tom, the "uncle", watches on, she will, however, take swift and fierce revenge.

Beyond the detective quest and the love story, *The Wreck* is thus a powerful psychological portrait of the ways in which an innocent young girl can be groomed, manipulated, seduced by a powerful older male relative using a mixture of fear, force, and adult authority to obtain compliance. It points to the cycles of precocious sexualization and attachment that such abuse of sexual power can give rise to, as Léna's story of incestuous violence is repeated, spiralling through webs of forbidden relationships, forward to future generations and back to a founding myth, re-constructed here by Gorodé as the shipwreck that results in a young girl being cast away with her grandfather. Although Léna's great grandmother has powers as an ogress, and although Éva holds the power of exorcism, it is childhood memories of victimization that, above all, connect Maria, Lila, Helena and Léna. It is hardly surprising that all the female Kanak characters subsequently remain prey to violent oscillation between shame and passionate fascination in their adult amorous encounters.

These shared experiences of childhood rape and resulting adult sexual possession by their aggressor allow the lives of the generations of women, of Helena's (Ogress) grandmother, of Helena (Old Léna), of young (Hé)Léna, of her daughter, little Léna, to morph one into the other, as did the five generations of young women, all named Ute Mûrûnû, in Gorodé's earlier novella. Among male characters, incestuous relations, predilection for young girls, rape, and male animal magnetism likewise cause the two 'fishermen' (Old Tom and the orator) to morph.

Moreover, in Gorodé's fictional identification of the differences that constitute Kanak identity – that set her characters apart from the conventional, European fictional individuals characterized by unique, memorable, and developing personalities – it is precisely these spiralling inter-relationships that remain central. In Kanak culture, as Gorodé points out, every fourth generation is considered to replace its forbear, and carry the same name (homonym).

The novel opens with young Tom recounting a dream of the ancestor, the spirit of canoes, to his cousin. Such dreams reinforce the sense of spiralling time, of a return of the past in the present. They also deepen the ambiguities surrounding the roles of the ancestors, the uses of *mana* for good and for evil, and the power of "black magic" – of Old Tom, like the totem, as a figure of, on the one hand, of wisdom, power and protection and, on the other, of danger and abuse. Pursued by a shark fin and swimming toward a canoe in danger of being wrecked, where an old fisherman is stretching out his hand, Tom sees the canoe transform into the black rock. Tom's cousin, who had himself dreamt of a fisherman near a canoe with a young girl inside it, tells Tom that the old fisherman is the ancestor issuing a premonitory warning. The dream also constitutes a *mise en abyme*, an internal duplication, of the thematic elements, in particular the wreck. Its various metamorphoses will construct the metaphoric backbone of the tale.

(Da)lila, also a natural daughter of Old Tom, raped by her "father" and father's brothers up in the mining centre over "a thousand years of suffering and shame" describes herself as a literal wreck, "a heart of stone in a human body adrift for life". She has run away from her abusive family, ending up on the streets of Nouméa, a colourful figure of the bar scene with her constant story-telling. Like Helena, Maria and Éva, playful figures of the myths of the doubleness of woman as *femme fatale*, angel and devil, (Da)lila frequents the libertine, Old Tom, and his friends in the wreck of the colonial ship, *Fleur de Corail* [Coral Flower], whose overturned hull pulled up on the beach shelters the love-making, over generations, of both Old and young Tom.

This wrecked boat-hull is, in its turn, a variant of the prow-shaped rock of the ancestral canoe in the canoe-graveyard up in the *tribu*. A canoe and a yacht of equal size (almost certainly a coded image for the *Accords de Nouméa*) under the glass counter in the old settlers' small beach-side shop in Nouméa, with its walls covered by historical images of boats, from the Roman galley to the steam-ship, point similarly to a certain self-conscious and self-reflexive functioning of a text deliberately strewn with the wreckage of history.

The repetition of the language of possession similarly paints all of the novel's detailed and repeated descriptions of (often perverse) games of love with the irony of stereotypical metaphor, as waves rise and break thunderously making their seminal offerings, and the young couple sail away on "tormented seas" or to "island paradises". A series of female characters wriggle like worms on the ground, in submission under the predatory boot or big toe of Old Tom and the orator (an ironic allusion to the early anthropological theories of the distinctively adroit Melanesian big toe) but also, to even things out, of the philandering white colonial sea-captain, widely rumoured to be the natural father of his young mistress.

On a more serious level, however, like the omnipresent figures of incest, the questions of the pleasure of the body and of women's role in their own enslavement represent the *non-dit*, the unspoken, of the Kanak world. Rejecting an over-idealized image of customary Kanak life, and questioning the cult of *mana* as male virility – as it is perpetuated in Jean-Marie Tjibaou's mobilization of Kanaké as emblematic founding figure, in order to create a suddenly single Kanak culture – Gorodé's novel presents a challenge to Tjibaou's phallocratic and idealized national model.

The details of the outlawed nocturnal ecstasy shared by Maria and Éva as Old Tom sleeps, or by Léna and Éva in Éva's paradisical garden, make an indirect case for the existence of, and the right to, female physical pleasure, a pleasure that Éva claims is one that can also be freely given "without constraint or possession". The repeated, explicit and apparently gratuitous descriptions of shocking sexual encounters or lesbian sexual pleasure go beyond what might also be labelled a writing experiment in *jouissance*, the metaphorical pleasure of the text, or indeed, of an exploration of the uncanny of the female sexual body, its bodily fluids and reproductive functions that Kanak tradition, like so many others, has proscribed as dangerous and taboo. The sexually free Éva, who creates an interface between the patriarchal tribe and modernity, an independent space where she nonetheless continues to respect the customary values of sharing and solidarity, also represents women's knowledge, "an immense knowledge, as old as the world. An immeasurable power, as free as the wind".

However, the presence of vengeful or malevolent figures of female occult power – the witch, or the Ogress, for example, "looking for a little girl to take with her on the wreck, far, far away over the stormy seas", for fresh meat to feed to the cannibal Ogre – obviate any uncomplicated understanding of the feminine. Female complicity in exploitative patriarchal authority within the village pose problems for Helena and her "homonym" Léna in the next generation. At the same time, the two women retain aspects of their stereotypical classical namesake, the beautiful and fateful Helen of Troy. Both Helena (Old Léna) – who runs off as an adolescent to Nouméa with Old Tom later returning to the *tribu* to be with the orator in another forbidden relationship – and young Léna – who plays willing sexual victim in a taboo threesome with the orator and Helena – assume a certain disruptive power as highly sexual, non-wifely, non-maternal, women. A certain undecideability or "cognitive dissonance", as we noted earlier, complicates the reading of these both victimized (passive) and victimizing (active) characters.

The powers of seduction of Old Tom and his natural son, the orator, promiscuous and potent fishermen, misusing their authority, particularly adept at gathering little girls in their nets and, as Éva puts it, "attaching their bellies", by violence, on the black stone in the ancestral graveyard, similarly argue for a rethinking of Custom that goes beyond the self-evident denunciation of child sexual abuse into the territories of the workings of power: gender relations and sexual politics.

Clear critical or didactic voices do emerge speaking, for example, of the gap between the elevated and male-dominated Word, together with the hierarchies and rites of tradition that bear it, and what goes on unseen and unspoken "in the hay and under the mimosa bushes" or indeed, under the very eyes of the pastor at Church on Sundays. Narrative irony designates the hypocritical authority behind the formal role played by the orator, as bearer of the Word at the marriage ceremony, and his simultaneous illicit re-possession of Léna, against a tree, or later on the floor of his wife's thatch house, despite the watching ancestors on the doorposts. Éva tells Léna that sexuality is natural and should not be a cause for guilt or anxiety but should, nonetheless, be kept in its place, that is, in nature "there where it reigned triumphant. On the ground, in the mud, on the grass, against a tree or in the water... quite simply a part of the world into which we are born and given senses to explore".

For, Éva appears to have escaped from the possession of an earlier relationship with Old Tom that was "sending her mad" and assumes a posture of female agency, living a sexually independent life between Nouméa and the *tribu*, while still fulfilling her social obligations to the group. "She refused to submit to it. Absolutely refused. And most particularly because she felt that passion was an alienation, very like the power exerted by the sorcerer over his victim." And yet, subsequently afraid of hell-fire, Éva will join a sect, be seduced and cheated by the pastor, and will indeed end up in a psychiatric institution. Likewise, Lila, avatar of Gorodé, a story-teller re-inventing the tales of oral tradition from a modern female perspective to show both their contemporary relevance and their patriarchal origins, cannot escape the power of Old Tom. She will be raped and assassinated. But, despite representing Dalila, the stereotypical figure of the "betraying" feminine, and the product of language play, "Lila the barefoot Bardessa", "Lila the flower with the overpowering scent", like Éva, remains a voice for Kanak women's rights and social responsibilities.

In contrast to the unambiguous critique in *Utê Mûrûnû* of the imposition on Kanak women by the missionaries of the image of Eve bitten by the serpent, in *The Wreck*, the case for women's sexual liberation is not made without reserves. Indeed, one voice opens the text up to the claim that the worm is always, already, fatally, in the fruit – perhaps something to do with Old Tom's ancestral eating of the forbidden fruit (his daughter). As the quote from the Epistle to the Romans offered at Lila's funeral laments, "What fruit had ye then from those things whereof ye are now ashamed? For the end of those things is death." (*Romans* 6, v.23)

Éva and Maria's nightly trysts when the men were asleep are presented as a quest, but the repetition of cliché and the wording of the text again suggest that transcendence through sexuality, or indeed, through "the paradise of women" is an illusion. "These sisters of the 'second sex', one half of the sky, the salt of the earth, were sailing the seas of sensual pleasure and ecstasy, dancing the dance of hungry bellies in a quest for something sublime that must lie beyond the derisory illusions of orgasm."

Where does Gorodé herself stand in these stories of forbidden loves, infidelity, jealousy, revenge (the settler's wife's mysterious death in a car wreck that allows him to continue his illicit love relationship with a Kanak woman despite "colonial apartheid"), abuse, female masochism? Is it perhaps in Old Tom's sudden appearances and disappearances, his metamorphoses, coded language and linguistic playfulness that the writer's hand, her discursive strategies, are most clearly imaged? Like the figure of old Tom, Gorodé's text shifts constantly from one realm to another. Indeed, from his first appearance as a scarlet dwarf emerging out of the night fire with a putrid smell as little Helena watches her grandmother's astonishing show of absolute submission, Tom is a recognizable character both of fairy-tale, of fiction and of Pacific history. In Nadi airport, the portrait of "Cannibal Tom" is offered for sale to tourists along with the legend – and the salesgirl will tell you where to find the records of the number of the people he used to eat a day!

We noted that the horizons of expectation for readers of indigenous literature are somewhat pre-determined. An indigenous writer is by and large expected to produce testimonial narratives of cultural loss, exotic and/or ethnographic portraits of his/her community, and/or political manifestoes, often recounted by the voices of the group rather than of the individual. Although Gorodé's text is clearly a literary construction of the world and its meanings through a ludic play on genre and language, incorporating rap-songs, oral stories, and foundation myth in a kind of *bricolage*, it is nonetheless assumed it will largely follow conventions of plot, character and point of view conforming to European norms.

The Wreck does present a unique, ethnographic portrait of Kanak life, from the inside, including precise detail of the nature of cultural syncretism– for example, in the careful description of traditional, Christian and French marriage ceremonies rolled into one. The novel documents present socio-economic realities: the female characters all work as maids; the male characters either do gardening for "Whites", work in the mines, or are unemployed. Many scenes celebrate Kanak culture: the sharing shown in Éva's regular Sunday *bougna* (food cooked in an earth oven) for her extended family; the euphoria of the memories of the Kanak Popular School movement; the solidarity and purpose of the protest march for Independence. This march, itself a political *fête* that opens the novel, nonetheless slides into the Saturday commercial fair on the *Place des Cocotiers* and into other forms of modern celebration in the alcohol- and cannabis-filled bars of Nouméa, where Tom meets Léna. '*Fête*' (as later in the marriage festivities), like many of Gorodé's figures, can show both positive and degraded faces.

On the other hand, the novel's avowals also run counter to the expectations of its readers in a text that stages the need to go beyond "sharing as custom provides", beyond the façade of appearances. Gorodé has observed that in writing this novel, she sought to unmask the dangers for a Kanak society of hiding behind the image of a virtuous culture assimilated to an untouchable custom. Māori theorist, Linda Tuhiwai Smith, has similarly deconstructed the authentic, deeply spiritual indigenous Other and the idea of primitive, 'noble' original customary communities.[17] In addition, like Mme de Lafayette's subtle first French novel, *La Princesse de Clèves*, which conjoins a study of fatal attraction and the pull of duty (to others or to self), rather than placing them in opposition, the play of Gorodé's textual characters, as they engage with the powers of sexual sorcery, models psychological tension and moral complexity. At the same time, the non-wifely, highly sexual Éva, Helena, or Lila challenge myths of indigenous women. These figures are no South Seas maidens. In fact, Goode's work can be seen to be linked to an avant-garde tradition of writing/the transgressive liberation of love as a challenge to puritanical or bourgeois political regimes and their control of social mores. Other contemporary non Western writers such as Tarun Tejpal in India (*The Alchemy of Desire*) also escape from being pigeon-holed in the "exotic postcolonial" through the shock induced in the reader by their explicit and repeated description of sexual encounters.

Finally, there is not only thematic violence in this novel but also the discursive violence of clashing points of view (one narrator or generation can hide another) unstable narrators and shifting linguistic registers, cyclical repeating movement with sudden irruptions, verbal jousting and constant displacements: The European wreck on the beach in Nouméa that slides into the black rock of the canoe graveyard in the Kanak village, the *pirogue* of the ancestor that becomes the rock shaped like a canoe. Even if the uncle/orator who rapes the young Léna on the black rock shaped like a canoe is identified by the text with the destructive influence of colonization and cultural assimilation, Old Tom also recounts that he had been initiated into games of love by a polygamous Kanak grandfather who had resisted evangelization.

It is perhaps in its heterogeneous interweaving of thematic elements, voices, and levels of narration that Gorodé's message is constructed: in the excessive stories of prostitution, voyeurism, "games of three or four or more" in the wrecked hull of the old boat; on the paving-stones of the Church, in defiance, as the text itself points out, of the codes of both Christian and Customary morality; descriptions of games of master/mistress and slave, in which women are willing participants. The text ranges from the didactic to the ironic to the preposterous, from an exposé of dramatic social issues to a work on the ready-made expressions of the French language. These multiple voices both meet and foil the reader's expectations. They may, of course, also hide the more intimate personal memories and preoccupations that Gorodé's text is exploring, "unbeknownst" to her conscious self or public political persona.

The primal figure of the Ogre, Old Tom, the sorcerer ("Batman" in coded language), like the figure of the Ogress, sends back echoes of a European literary problematic of good and evil. Gorodé explicitly alludes to Stevenson's Dr Jekyll and Mr Hyde (as indeed to Jack the Ripper!), but Goethe's Faust, Othello, Beckett's human wrecks also come to mind. However, behind the interrogation in the novel of the mysteries concealed behind the traditional ceremonial mask or sacred stones – the ways in which they have been outlawed and altered under evangelization and colonialization – it is still the mask that continues to represent the Kanak way of life and tradition; continues to symbolize the close and not always reassuring presence of the other world that characterizes that life. Metamorphosis in *The Wreck* may still represent the moment when the human most powerfully channels the divine or the demonic. In any event, Gorodé insists that the stories presented in her text are not merely allegories but living history. For her, the Ogre, as incestuous uncle or cannibal father, is a social reality.

Each generation, Gorodé explains, "must resolve the return of the past in its own way".[18] In fact, the return staged by the last sentence of the novel, the encounter between the grandson of the orator, little Tom and Léna's daughter, little Léna, "in the grove of the great canoe where they learn to love on the black stone" may incorporate some optimism, despite its cyclical form. For although the children are the offspring of abusive relationships, their sexual initiation is consensual and suggests a new beginning. This is not linear progress or a closed circle but the spiral, spinning the "rope of man" as in Witi Ihimaera's work. "At the same time it is going out", says the Māori proverb, "it is returning." Likewise, here, at the same time as it is returning, it is going out.

Despite the necessary pirouettes of a writer and politician seeking to validate her culture but aware that this culture continues to oppress children and women, this novel is an "outing" of the problem of incest and sexual predation perpetuated across generations, and a manifesto for women's liberation and right to speak to a society in which sexual mores can be hypocritical and repressive of women's sexual bodies. Gorodé's *The Wreck* represents, a Kanak woman's singular and courageous attempt to use a literary work on language to tell the truth, braving the danger that this might be used against her (people).[19]

Translation Notes

As translators, our primary motivation has been respect for our author, for her people and culture, and for our readers. Translation always involves a process of re-writing and of negotiation. In walking the tightrope line between fidelity to the original and ensuring readability and comprehensibility, our assumption has been that our readers, as readers of Pacific fiction, will wish us to enable them to experience the original in all its singularity and strangeness.

We have thus sought to render, as faithfully as possible, Déwé Gorodé's unique style: her singular use of the French language which is at times idiosyncratic, at times classical; at times, lyrical, at times didactic. We have therefore preserved the many instances of non-standard tense use, rapid switches in register and syncopated rhythms of the original novel. In doing so, we hope to provide our readers with an experience that puts them into the shoes of the French-speaking audience, for whom *L'épave* is marked by both universal human drama and cultural difference.[20]

We have retained most culturally specific terms and proper nouns in the original French or Paicî (Déwé's first language), italicized to aid readability. We have included the author's footnotes and added our own translators' notes, to provide a gloss for cultural terms whose meaning is not clear from the context. In other cases, culturally specific items have been rendered by English equivalents. Thus for example, the centrally important term *la case* (traditional Kanak dwelling), is retained in the phrase *Grande Case* (with a pronunciation note and cultural information) but otherwise rendered descriptively as 'thatch-house', or more communicatively translated as "house" or "home".

Underlying many of our translation choices was the following question: If the author were writing in English, or addressing English-speaking readers of Pacific fiction, how would she have expressed things? For this reason, we chose to translate a number of terms from Kanak–French vernacular using Māori–Pasifika inflected English equivalents, as in the rap songs and poems that punctuate the novel. Thus, also, when translating from the French, *Mamie, grand-mère* and *grand-père*, we preferred Nanny and Pop, over the more standard, Anglo-Saxon-sounding Grandma and Grandad.

Our task was made easier, and infinitely more pleasant, by the fact that we were in regular contact with Déwé, and her comments were invaluable, both in clarifying meaning and in assisting us to make the most appropriate translation choices.

Our aim was always to respect the integrity of the novel and its author, while providing our readers with an experience that is at once aesthetically satisfying and both semantically and culturally authentic.

Deborah Walker-Morrison and Raylene Ramsay

Endnotes

1   Déwé Gorodé, *L'Epave*, Nouméa, Madrepores, 2005.

2   Parts of this section have been freely translated and adapted from the biographical notes appearing in an Appendix to the French edition of *L'épave*.

3   English editions have appeared as *The Kanak Apple Season*, edited and translated Peter Brown, Canberra: Pandanus Press, Australian National University, 2004 and of *Sharing as Custom Provides*, a collected anthology of poetry in bilingual form, translated and edited by Raylene Ramsay and Deborah Walker, Pandanus Press, 2005.

4   The *Code de l'Indigénat* was abolished in 1946.

5 Déwé Gorodé and Nicolas Kurtovich, *Dire le vrai / To Tell the Truth*, transl. Raylene Ramsay and Brian MacKay, Nouméa, Grain de Sable, 2000.

6 Talk by Déwé Gorodé at the University of Auckland in May 2006 on the occasion of the publication of *Sharing as Custom Provides.*

7 Adapted from *Sharing as Custom Provides*, pp. 148–49.

8 Déwé Gorodé, *Ûte Mûrûnû, petite fleur de cocotier*, Nouméa, Grain de sable, 1994. Extract translated by Deborah Walker, in *Nights of Storytelling. A cultural History of Kanaky-New Caledonia*, ed. R. Ramsay, Honululu, University of Hawaii Press, 2011.

9 Déwé Gorodé, *Pierre Noire*, Nouméa, Grain de Sable, 1997. Translation of the poems of Grace Mera Molisa in Black Stone, Suva, SPAS Mana Publications, 1983.

10 Christine Hamelin et Christine Salomon, «Parenté et violences faites aux femmes en Nouvelle-Calédonie. Un éclairage sur l'ethnicité différenciée des violences subies au sein de la famille», *Espace populations sociétés* [En ligne], 2004/2 | 2004 , mis en ligne le 21 septembre 2009, consulté le 14 avril 2011. URL : http://eps.revues.org/index195.html

11 *Sharing as Custom Provides*, p. 22

12 Patty O'Brien, *The Pacific Muse: Exotic femininity and the colonial Pacific, University of Washington Press, Seattle*, 2006.

13 Alan Duff, *Once Were Warriors*, Auckland, Tandem Press, 1990. Film adaptation, directed by Lee Tamahori, 1994.

14 Transcribed and translated from a talk by Déwé Gorodé at the University of Auckland, May 2006.

15 'Custom' in "Signs of the Times", *Sharing as Custom Provides*, p. 128.

16 *Sharing as Custom Provides*, p. 38.

17 Linda Tuhiwai Smith, *Decolonizing Mythologies, Research and Indigenous Peoples*, Dunedin: University of Otago Press, 1999.

18 Personal interview with Gorodé, 24 May 2006.

19 "Telling the truth" is both the title of the poem and of Gorodé's collection of poems, *Dire le vrai.*

20 For a detailed discussion of our translation approach, see D. Walker & R Ramsay, "Translating hybridity: the curious case of the first Kanak novel (Déwé Gorodé's *L'épave*)", *Aalitra*, Vol 1, Issue 1, March 2010, pp 36–51.

In memory of Marie-Paule from the Garrison squat
For Éva, Maria, Lila, Léna
And so many others
For Tom and Léna

A woman's most becoming adornment is silence
  Sophocles, Ajax, *verse 293*

Chapter 1 – Big Day Out

Tom is swimming for his life to escape the pursuing fin, swimming towards the outrigger canoe of a solitary old fisherman as it bobs and sways on a choppy sea and lurches dangerously close to a rocky outcrop where it is about to founder. The moment the old man reaches out a hand to pull him aboard, his hand sticks fast to Tom's and the canoe is transformed into a wreck and a black rock. Tom screams in horror, a cry that is in fact no more than a closed-mouth sigh on a face that tenses at the touch of the first dawn light. He wakes with a start, turns over, props himself on one elbow and looks over at his young cousin sleeping soundly on the other mattress in the studio apartment. Realising that he had been dreaming, or rather, having a nightmare, he pushes back the blanket and goes over to the sink to throw cold water on his face. He fills a pot with water and puts it on the gas stove to boil. He brushes his teeth and when he comes back, towel over one shoulder, to the sound of the water boiling, his cousin is stretching awake. Rubbing the sleep from his eyes, he tells Tom he has just seen him walking along a beach toward an old fisherman who lives there, near a wreck where a young girl lies sleeping.

— That's funny, me too, just before I got up, I dreamt about an old fisherman, only in a canoe out on a stormy sea. And then, the ancestor grabbed me.

— What ancestor?

— Him, the fisherman. He's an ancestor that sticks to your skin.

— What d'you mean?

— I mean the palm of his hand stuck to mine. Like glue.

— An ancestor in a canoe sticking to you like glue. Yeah, that's the one Nanny calls the canoe-spirit.

— Whoever he is, this canoe-spirit really put the wind up me. I was screaming just before I woke up. And I was swimming like hell to get away from this black fin that was after me.

— Maybe he's come to tell us something, seeing as how I saw him too.

— How d'you mean?

— Well, the old fisherman by the wreck with the little girl asleep in it, that's him too.

— Oh, so you think he's the same one I saw?

— Yeah, the fin and the fisherman, they're one and the same. It's him. The ancestor. The canoe-spirit. And actually, he closed in on you cos you were trying to get away from him. But he appeared to us both, just to be sure.

— Sure of what?

— That we get the message he has for us.

— And just what would this message be, in your opinion?

— Tom, I think it's about you. You need to watch out for yourself.

— Look, it's just dreams.

— True. But as Nanny says, that's how and where they speak to us. Dreams are their world and their way of communicating. But if you want to take it that way...

— What I mean is, we've got other fish to fry in the land of the living, right? Specially today. So, first we get ourselves a good coffee. Next, you get your civvies on. Then we head on down to the demo.

—What I'm trying to say is – it's us, their descendants. Us, their grandchildren and great-grandchildren. Us in the land of the living before we die and go and join them. Or us, the living, with them here inside of us.

— Listen, cuz, we've got our whole lives ahead of us before we go and join our ancestors for eternity. Yeah, we got plenty of time, seeing as how they're here, inside of us, like you say.

— That's just it. They're inside of you and they're protecting you, in the here and now. Not after, when we're with them on the other side, cos by then we won't need protecting.

— Hang on, cuz. All I'm saying is, we've got all the time in the world to talk about it. So we'll talk about it later on, OK?

— Fine by me. But I'm not sure we've got all the time in the world. What if we run into a problem around the corner, when we leave here? And anyway, seeing as they have all eternity, why d'you think they're appearing to us now, if not to warn us or put us on our guard?

— All right, all right, cuz. Gotcha. I'll look out. So where's the meeting place for the demo?

— Usual place.

— Where's the march starting from?

— Same place, down along the sea front.

— OK. Be good to meet up with the bros.

And they're all there, the bros, the pops and the grandpops, the sisters, the mamas and the grandmas, comrades, mates and relations making up the extended family. The years have brought with them spouses, partners and children, sharing the same hopes, the same unfailing determination. Welcomes are sung out to the beat of kanaka music over the loudspeakers as the protest marchers arrive in a steady flow. They come on foot, by car, bus and taxi. From downtown, from the four corners of the city, from the villages and tribes, they answer the call of the movement fighting against exploitation and domination in all its forms. Fighting for freedom, for justice, for dignity.

Brothers born of long years of common struggle, the organisers meet and greet each other, and begin discussing details of the demands to be made in the speeches. Some deliberate as to what protocol should be observed, the customary gestures that must be made to the local clans before speaking, singing, or setting foot on their soil. Speaking the link to the land. Others organise the banners and distribute placards and marshals' badges. Others again keep a tally of who's there and who's not. The loudspeakers alternate marching instructions and music: Melanesian, Polynesian, Caribbean, African, in the original language or in English, Pidgin, or French. They are setting the tone for the Big March on the tarseal of the town. The cops stop the traffic to allow the march to begin, as motorists look on and as TV cameras and news photographers prowl, on the look out for the shot of the day or the shot of the century to sell later to the highest bidder.

The party leaders and elected representatives lead the march arm in arm under the Kanaky flag, taking up the whole road. A giant placard at the head of the march pays tribute to all the exploited peoples of the planet in their ongoing struggle for dignity and a better quality of life. This march is part of the continuous struggle to beat the odds of a system stacked against them. The oppressed of the world are blinded to the true nature of the global market vampire that bleeds them dry. It appeals to them like a sky stuffed full of gods offering false promises to the colonised.

The marchers stream past in a steady rhythm, picking up and chanting the slogans that are shouted out between songs from the loudspeakers, in a single resolute voice. The women follow on, laughing and swapping gossip as they march. Those who haven't seen each other in a while seize the opportunity to catch up with old friends, and their children, marching by their side, are happy to see their former classmates again. And so the long protest line advances slowly but surely through the streets of the town.

Tom meets up with brothers, cousins and female relations from his tribe up north in the mountains across the Central Divide who have come to Noumea specially for the march. Their presence takes him back to his childhood – memories of the schoolyard, of diving off the rocks or fishing for shrimp, loach-fish and eels in the creek. They talk about the mandarin season when, at dusk, they'd light the fire

4

that warms body and soul at storytelling time in the *Grande Case*[1], or of the long silent walks through the bush when they would join the men hunting *roussettes*,[2] *notou* pigeons,[3] wild pigs and deer. He thinks back to the smell of the forest, the taste of honey and roasted *bancoule* grubs[4] dug out of tree trunks and fallen logs. He remembers the perfume of *niaouli*[5] flowers and *tabou* wood and the unexpected beauty of wild orchids.

The rhythm of the march and the chanting of slogans remind the marchers of the first meetings of the movement back home in the village, organised by the young people of back then, one of whom is among the leaders in the front row today. They march with the same enthusiasm, the same dignity, the same determination; with the same clear, simple, convincing voice that won a few old stalwarts of the colonial status quo over to their cause; with the same commitment that led the people to stake their land claims and begin political action on the barricades during the 'Troubles', under the control of party cells working towards a common purpose. They think back to the first time the Kanaky flag was raised, by an old grandfather who had the same measured gestures as the present leader, whose voice carried the same unequivocal truth. It was Tom's own grandfather, in

---

1   *Grande Case* (pronounced 'kaze'). In the traditional Kanak village, the *Grande Case* is a symbol of the clan and of chiefly power. A tall conical building of thatch, it is supported by a central pole hewn from the trunk of a great tree. Set on a mound (tertre), the *Grande Case* is approached along a ceremonial pathway lined with rows of columnar pines and coconut palms. The lawn in front of the *Case*, and the pathway are places of meeting and discussion. The back of the *Case* is the realm of the enigmatic world of the spirits, the ancestors and their powers. (Transl.)

2   Flying foxes (*Pteropus ornatus*). (Transl.)

3   New-Caledonian imperial Pigeon (*Ducula goliath*), *déa-tuu*, in Paicî. (Transl.)

4   Larva (*Agrianome fairmairei*), living in a dead bancoule tree (*Aleurites moluccana*). (Transl.)

5   *Melaleuca quinquenervia*. (Transl.)

fact – an old clan chief who has always offered his crucial, unwavering support.

And then, inside of Tom, they are there. His mother and father. They are still with him and will always be there with him. Alive as ever in his memory. They blend into memories of the *tribu*, that small corner of earth where he took his first steps and where, one day, he will lie again. He is what he is through what they made of him. They took upon themselves everything that might have weighed him down. The burdens of life. The weight of existence. And took it all away when they left him, when they were killed in the accident. Tom left too, not long after, for the army.

After the leaders have presented their official list of demands to the authorities, the procession returns to its starting point and the march breaks up. The marchers head off in different directions through the town. As today is also a 'Saturday shopping fest', the city streets are decked out with garlands and banners. Everybody's on the lookout for the bargain of a lifetime, anything from a multicoloured beach ball to a reconditioned old car. Kids with their faces painted to look like cats, dogs or owls run around lighting firecrackers and firing water-pistols at imaginary bandits. Teenagers are checking out T-shirts, jeans and sneakers. Young girls try on lipstick, mascara, nail polish. Women pore over the prices of pots and pans, crockery and household items. Mums are busy perusing potted orchids, Colombo plants and cordylines, while dads linger in front of lawnmowers, weedeaters, rotary-hoes. The stallholders unpack their wares – stacking, displaying, covering the pavement with anything and everything they can possibly sell. The customers think twice, adding up, counting their pennies. Everybody's calculating to the max.

Except, that is, for the ones among the crowd who couldn't give a hoot for all this showy display of merchandise. The dead-broke ones who have just come to look around, have a wander, check it out. They wait for mates with a few spare bucks to shout them a drink, a coffee or a meal or takeaways from one of the many foodstalls: spring rolls, meatballs, sandwiches, that they can sit on the grass and eat. Others have trouble finding a spot for themselves on the lawn between the bodies sitting or lying around in groups, talking, eating, and sleeping. But the constant movement of people passing by, coming and going continuously through the streets and gardens, seems to lead all and sundry off on some preset path, pounding the pavement in search of the ultimate object of desire. The narrow confines of the town centre are awash in the festive atmosphere that makes everyone want to move, mosey, go with the flow. The crowd mills around the town in a kind of magic merry-go-round, the hordes of noisy kids having a ball, oblivious to their parents. Everyday cares and woes dissolve away in the general euphoria; all the problems of the world appear to have been put aside by common consensus. And for those who are still having trouble keeping up or who can't chill out, even for a few hours, there'll always be plenty of good mates to get them drunk or stoned. For the regulars, this Saturday shopping fest means double the usual number of cans of beer and cartons of cheap red wine or free booze, taking them even higher, crazier, drunk beyond their wildest dreams.

Tom's cousin, who has become separated from him during the march, manages to catch up with Léna, the girl he's been dating, though somewhat chastely, for a number of weeks now. Léna abandons the two cousins who had joined her for the protest and goes off with him. She appreciates the young man's quiet manner: she's not long lost her mother and is not in the mood for casual relationships. He's in the middle of doing his army service and, since he's on guard duty later this evening, he has to be back at the barracks quite early. But he also wants to find Tom and introduce Léna to him. They have chow mein and fried rice at a little Vietnamese place and are about to sit down for a chat in a busy café when Tom comes in with a girlfriend who happens to know Léna and who introduces them. Dressed in his Hawaiian shirt and smiling, Tom offers a friendly handshake all round and sits down opposite Léna. They order a round of drinks then launch into a conversation that Léna has trouble following at first, what with the noise of the pool tables and pinball machines, the laughter coming from the next table and the sharp humour of Tom's girlfriend, who has everyone in fits.

Next thing, Léna hears her saying:

— *It's a story about a fisherman grappling with a big catch on the end of his line, so big it pulls his canoe behind it for an entire night along the length of a wide bay. At dawn, shock number one! He finds himself back on the beach, sitting in front of the biggest fish he's ever caught. With his axe he hacks a doorway into its belly that he then explores with a torch. And then, shock number two! He's in the biggest coconut plantation he's ever seen, with an endless supply of coconut milk. He walks on cautiously, driven by a mixture of curiosity and fear. And then, shock number three! An enormous woman, with a skirt and hair made of coconut fronds, a coconut trunk for a body, with coconuts for breasts and eyes, is lying before him on a gigantic mat. 'Come and have a drink from my coconuts, little man,' she whispers and her voice is like the wind that blows him between her breasts. 'Come on, take hold of my two coconuts and have a drink. You know how. Go on, little man, don't be afraid. Two good coconuts, just like the ones you drink every day! Help yourself, little man!' He does as she says and suckles at her two coconuts as if she were his mother. He suckles and suckles and finally falls asleep like a baby between her two breasts. A long time after, as if at the end of a dream, he hears her voice, a whispering wind that says, 'Farewell, little man, you're a big boy now. You are truly a man.' And there he is, back on the beach, under the coconut palms, in the place where the big fish landed his canoe. And then, final shock! No fish. No woman... Gone!*

At regular intervals, people they know come in, say hello, sit down next to their table or move on. The hustle and bustle of people from the surrounding boutiques and shops winds its way into the café and out the other side again, back onto the street. With all this commotion, Léna can't really make out what anyone's saying except for Tom, who

8

has conveniently opted to address her exclusively, since she's sitting opposite him. But from time to time, it's the girlfriend's voice that dominates. She has the gift of the gab and a whole repertoire of funny stories that are a perfect fit for a day such as this. As she tells one story after another, Tom and Léna are in tears, looking into each other's eyes. Between peals of laughter, unbeknownst to them all, something starts between the two of them; they turn away momentarily to look at the storyteller then back at each other while they listen to her tale:

— *This one's about a man who boasts of owning a taro field containing every species of taro that exists. Ones for eating, ones for planting, medicinal ones and ones you exchange. Soon his taros produce so many shoots, sprouts and cuttings that he can't remember their names and ends up completely lost and confused. The mountain taro ends up in the place where the water taro should be and vice versa.*
— *What are you doing down there in the water, mountain-taro?*
— *I am drowning, water-taro.*
— *What are you doing up there on dry land, water-taro?*
— *I am dying, mountain-taro.*
— *And so, the collector's taros perish. In wanting to possess them all, the man ends up losing them all.*

She continues like this, captivating an audience that comes and goes, gathering around their small, round table topped with an ashtray that is steadily filling with butts and cigarette ash. An audience that has completely lost interest in the rowdy joyous spectacle that fills the rest of the room and the street outside.

Tom and Léna are drifting now, borne along by their friend's stories like two twigs, two wrecks drawn irresistibly together at the whim of an unfathomable current that binds them one to the other as they career headlong towards some enchanted atoll, some tortured ocean. Each one floats, hopelessly adrift in the other's amused gaze, carried away by the magical spontaneity of laughter. Like two enchanted children at a puppet show. For each of them, the telling of the stories is an exploration of the contours of a face, the meaning of a smile, the depths of a gaze. For each, the narration follows the lobe of an ear, brushes against a cheek, lingers at the nape of a neck. In this way, the storyteller's tale, her humour and her entertainer's art, serve the dual purpose of exposing and concealing the signs of an irreversible intimacy: tying the inextricable threads that will weave the story of a new couple waiting in the wings, about to be born, unbeknownst to all,

Towards mid afternoon, doubtless weary of amusing her audience with this kind of repertoire – a therapy as absurd as it was unnecessary, given the euphoric reality of the day itself – the storyteller finishes her act on a slightly more ironic note.

— It's the story of a little girl who got pinched during the night by a big crab. Ever since, she can't stop catching crabs down in the mangroves. And every time she eats one, she feels a sharp pain, in the place where the crab pinched her. To stop the pain, she resists the call of the crabs and decides to stop fishing for them in the mangroves. But that night, she hears them crawling up towards her, so she goes and stands by the hearth with her back to the fire, facing the door. The big crab arrives, comes in and makes straight for her. The moment he goes to grab her between his claws, she moves sideways and the big crab falls into the fire, pinching at the embers.

Then the storyteller, like some disillusioned diva or world-weary star who must fly off to some other, infinitely more important engagement, proclaims that, having still more sales and bargain-hunting to do, she must leave them. Nonetheless, and with no illusions as to the answer, she asks Tom what he's planning to do. He announces that he's staying, as if to say 'too late'.

He is older than both Léna and his cousin, so he takes the lead in organising the rest of the afternoon. He starts by taking them out of the café whose magic spell, now broken by the end of the funny stories and the laughter, had allowed him to see himself reflected in the gaze of the young girl whose serenity now reminds him of the calm preceding the storm. He takes the other two for a short walk, his stride adopting the continuous movement of the carnival crowd so that they have no trouble keeping up as he leads them on a kind of enchanted wander, weaving through streets that have thrown off their usual sleazy rags and put on their party clothes, the myriad patterns and shades of which multiply with every step they take. On this extraordinary walk, they each savour what captures their gaze and their fancy in the orgy of colours and manufactured goods. Made in Japan, China, Taiwan and all those other mythical places of origin, in factories making mass-produced goods, ready to take production straight offshore, where, from the weaving to the printing, they make the symbols of our identity: Kanaky flags by the hundreds, or whatever you care to order. In this joyous, whirling dance, a furtive glance from beneath a blue-shadowed eyelid, out from a mass of dreadlocks or finely braided extensions, sets off the wildest imaginings. The three friends allow themselves to be carried off toward other dreams, like those others who, only the day before or that same morning, at the first light of dawn, had laid down their protest demands on behalf of all those who are excluded from the money economy of the merchant town; written them out on banners carefully spread beneath the leafy branches of a false pepper tree, somewhere on the other side of the hills. Now that they've shifted their beggar's bag onto the other shoulder or hung it up in a shanty hut down by the mangroves, the protesters can let themselves go, be drawn into the delicious whirlwind of the day's festivities and live it up. Happily putting aside the militant fervour of the morning, they give themselves, body and soul, to the wave of light-hearted pleasure that carries them toward more carefree shores. In this magical journey into the beating heart of shopping land, into the pulsing lungs of the city's market economy, off they go, hearts on fire and bodies in a trance, toward other shores, other desires, other pleasures.

Tom is suddenly gripped by an amazing burst of activity, an incredible surge of energy: like some multihull helmsman or a street entertainer, he gleefully drags the young couple from pavement to pavement, avenue to avenue, from one square to another. He is overflowing with a vitality that is every bit as sudden as it is surprising, but which is so perfectly in tune with the fever-hot atmosphere of the afternoon that it leaves little room for introspection. But there, on a street corner, hanging on a rack on the pavement, a pleated grey mission dress with white flowers suddenly forces upon him a distant vision of his mother, back home in the village up in the hills, amidst the columnar pines and fern-covered slopes. He would have liked to have given it to her as a gift, as he often used to do. He can't resist, and buys it. The assistant hands him his parcel, gift-wrapped, decorated with a little crêpe-paper rosette of black petals surrounding a tiny red heart that he spontaneously removes and pins on Léna's dress. She is moved by this sudden gesture, but all three nonetheless find it quite natural, in accordance with custom. Then, brushing a surreptitious hand against the nape of her neck as he pushes the parcel into her hand, he continues to guide them forward through the crowd.

They pass groups of young men having a good time, groups of girls laughing and joking among themselves. They make way for elegant women dressed in silk mission dresses, chatting quietly as they stroke a scarf or hand a sweet to a chubby-cheeked child, unmindful of the hustle and bustle of the crowded streets around them. They pass ladies with bleached, straightened hair, lashes thick with mascara, powdered cheeks and bright lipstick, their hips swaying as they sashay past, some in shorts, others in jeans and boots or high-heels. There is a growing warmth and intensity in the gaze of each passer-by as the minutes and hours tick away on watches that no one looks at, the better to lose all notion of time. Time and notions: emotions that, in no time at all, a rapper in the town square brings back into focus, quick as a flash, in perfectly measured rhythms and flowing rhymes, standing in the middle of a circle where he is joined by two or three pirouetting hip-hop dancers and break-dancers, rapping out his words in a two–three beat.

Brotha in struggle / Kanak bro / Caledo / from Oceania / Rasta / Wearin' dreads / wearin' extensions / Bob in yo' heart / he singin' / 'no woman / no cry' / Kanak sista / from Oceania / Islanda / don't ya cry now / don't cry Ma / my rebel song / won't last long / like our sorrows / no tomorrows / for our dead / like I said / mates in arms / comrade brothas / gotta be leaders / gotta stand tall / gotta fight see / for our dignity / for liberty / justice and equality / trod down / to the ground / this global trip / everywhere you look / global domination / global uniformity / by the bomb / heavy artillery / got the net / internet school now / so I learn / and I dance / and I sing / sing my song / sing my roots / they so long / rebel song / sing for dignity / for liberty / justice and equality / on my Island / Isle of Light / Light me home / Home my Land / Land my Tribe / Tribe my Nation / my Country / Kanaky.

And the rapper's words stay with them, their ears still ring with his music and their feet walk to its beat as they follow another happy group of afternoon revellers towards the dimmed lights of a bar, where a couple dances drunkenly, lost in a wild gyrating *tamuré*. The woman is the storyteller friend and now she ignores them.

Tom sits down on a stool at a low table. Opposite, Léna and his cousin sit side by side on a long black leather-backed sofa, whose other occupants are already pretty drunk – laughing and falling into strange bouts of stupor shaken by restrained sobs. Others sniffle, their voices weepy. Cigarette smoke, the smell of ash and butts and grass, make things and people look even blurrier, more dubious. In the rather murky atmosphere, Tom's presence highlights the quiet, childlike serenity that emanates from the young couple accompanying him – or should that be accompanied by him; he doesn't know which and anyway he doesn't really care, he's been in such a good space since they met up at the café. He feels like an elderly chaperone charged with watching over two chaste young fiancés. They look like two lost cherubs about to wander into the ogre's lair, and the idea of dumping them there so that he can go off and let his hair down with his usual mates doesn't even occur to him.

He wants to stay with them, end this day with them, with no thought of the night that will soon be here, let alone of tomorrow.

If he had momentarily succumbed to Léna's laughing gaze, lost himself in it for the duration of their friend's storytelling, he's quite sure he can forget about all that now. Especially since, right now, she seems a bit distant. And the events of the afternoon, the intoxicating atmosphere of the streets, their brief wandering, his suddenly renewed vitality, all this time spent in their company has gradually locked him into the role of elder brother. A role that suits him just fine, though the young couple seem quite in control of themselves. In the crowded closeness of this darkened bar where the music is a mixture of Polynesian, Melanesian and Caribbean and the drinks flow like the music, from the beer's bitter frothiness to the sharp lash of rum and the sweet aniseed flavour of pastis, the Olympian calm of his two protégés prevents him from letting himself go and sliding into one of those mammoth binges that he and his mates are well known for. Still, he has always been very aware of the anti-drugs and AIDS campaigns, always taken great care not to give in to the temptation of the odd joint or unsafe sex. He got into the habit of always using a condom during his long stint in the army. He had done a tour of duty with the UN forces in Europe and Africa, fighting fratricides and genocides cunningly orchestrated and twisted by the media into 'civil wars', 'inter-ethnic or inter-community conflicts' or other, more palatable euphemisms. Back then, when he was away somewhere, in Sarajevo, former Yugoslavia or in Kigali, Rwanda, his brothers and cousins back home in the *tribu* would tune in every morning at five to the TV news on France 2, hoping to maybe get a glimpse of him: an anonymous face, standardised, trivialised, sandwiched between other images and comments about snipers and 'Radio of a thousand hills', the racist Rwandan station.

Though it hasn't earned him the reputation of being a ladies' man, he has sometimes, found himself waking, surprised and dazed, in the early hours of the morning, lying flat on his stomach, on his back or on his knees, in the arms or expert hands of some one-night stand. Sometimes, he has woken to find himself lying on the steamy pillow of some second-rate hotel, or on a mattress on the worm-eaten floorboards of some old colonial villa squat. Or on a slab of dusty, sexless concrete under a crane on some construction site. Sometimes, he has woken choking on the frayed rectangle of a threadbare rug on the earthen floor of some shanty hut, under a cloud of factory dust. Or on the burning hot, dry grass on an arid hillside, under the mimosas. And in all of these places of casual encounters, he would hear a voice inside him, mocking and full of knowing irony, always asking the same question: 'Well, man, what the hell've you got yourself into this time, eh?' And so he'd shake himself out of it, throw some clothes on, clean himself up as best he could and get out of there quick smart. If the woman was an early riser, he would make up some urgent Sunday errand, giving her no time to think about maybe seeing him again. One of these women, after a night that had seemed, shall we say, promising, had happened to bump into him in a bar the next evening in full flirt with another woman, and told him what she thought of him. 'Asshole! You're barely out of my bed, my sheets are still warm and here you are ready to bang this bitch! I don't believe it, you've really got a nerve, mate! Anyway, who cares, go on, you can hump her and every other slut in town, I don't give a fuck, you dirty horny bastard!'

That time, while his other prospect made a quick getaway, he tried to calm the woman down, asking quietly, 'Hey, what's with you, babe? Haven't you got a husband somewhere? You better watch it, if he catches you here bawling me out, or somebody goes and tells him about it, you'll be in for a hiding!' She'd come back at him, yelling out for the whole room to hear: 'What? You hear what this little shithead's tryin' on? Reckons he's gonna tell my mate. Gonna blackmail me, you lowlife! Fuck it; you're all a bunch of macho assholes! And bloody fuckin' blackmailers as well. Just forget it! I don't believe it, I just don't fuckin' believe it...' And then she had burst into tears, and vanished into the night. The friend he was with asked, 'What's with you, man, going with a married woman, don't you know they're the worst

15

trouble?' And before he had the time or the gumption to think up a response, an old barfly sitting nearby joined in, slurring, 'Yeah, right but don't forget, on the other hand it's safer, cos if you get them up the duff, the kid'll still be recognised by the father if he doesn't know. Never fails. Every time a coconut! And you, my man, white as snow, home and hosed, right?' But his sleazy laughter is soon drowned out by the music and noise of the bar.

The storyteller friend is there and ignores them. Intrigued by the over-the-top craziness of the place, people dancing, arms waving, bumping into one another, swaying dangerously around under the cover of the half-lit, smoke-filled bar, heavy with the bitter-sweet smell of cannabis, Léna too seems to have forgotten the shared laughter that, for the first time and without her realising it, had shown her how to read a face. The end of the stories, the carnival atmosphere of the streets, now the semi-darkness broken by a few coloured spotlights against the comic background of this drinking house, take back one by one the laughing features of this face. As the hours pass, more drinkers and partygoers crowd in, so that the room becomes way too small and the atmosphere increasingly grotesque. Léna can't make out anything, no telltale note in this elder brother-like voice that addresses them as if they were good little children. And yet, when they met before in the café, it's the first time she'd really laughed since she lost her mum. Her mother's death had left her locked away with an unbearable sense of loss; ever since she passed away on that deathbed with its too-clean sheets, in that hospital with its too-white walls. She had been loaded like a white-wrapped parcel onto a stretcher that glided away on its tiny black wheels like one of those supermarket trolleys laden with biodegradable products, or an airport trolley carrying its load of lifeless luggage. That thin body, lying like a broken doll under those immaculate sheets, belonged to her mother. She had still been in good health at the time of the last yam harvest, but halfway through her fortieth year she had been eaten alive, devoured by a sudden and vicious cancer. A few days earlier her mother had told her that she had clearly seen the doctors and overheard them discussing this same body during her operation. 'I could see them and hear them all right, while they were cutting me up, and, ever since, my bellybutton's been bleeding and oozing,' she said softly, as if she wanted to leave her this final message as a painful inheritance. As if she wanted her daughter to understand the full meaning of her death, the full extent of her shame and humiliation at having been forced to put her self, the flesh of her body under the scalpels and the knives and all their other cutting tools. As the clean white uniforms, like strange ghosts, busied themselves with her mother's body, Léna clasped her cold, dead feet in a desperate embrace, shouting at them with all the violence repressed since those rare and final confessions, 'No, no! You cut her up. You're the ones that killed her. Leave her, leave her alone now! Can't you bloody leave her in peace! My mother's dead! Can't you see my mother's dead? Can't you hear me? Dead, dead, dead! Well and truly bloody dead! You all happy now? Leave her alone and get out! Get the hell out! Leave my mother in peace!'

One of her other mums, the one she was named after, Léna, was there to take her into her arms and calm her down, and just at that moment she had realised that one morning, a long time before her mother's illness was diagnosed, she had dreamed about this same hospital room, its walls entirely covered in white sheets and decked out with funeral wreaths. And she cried even harder. A long time after the burial and the customary mourning rituals, she was still haunted by her mother's shared confidence about being cut open while still conscious, and by the horrible image of her sewn-up body, lifeless now, ice-cold and stiff and hunched up under the bleached, starched sheets of this nightmare room with its floating smell of disinfectant.

She had been drifting around in this state of depression, submerged by grief in a solitude peopled with memories of her mother, when Tom's cousin had turned up. She had first met him years before, at a high-school exam. Struck by his steady, caring nature, so completely different from the usual insolent arrogance of boys of his age, she had allowed a friendship to develop, and so, when they met up again

17

by chance at this critical period in her life, she had not hesitated to let him console her. At this stage, though, she had no thoughts of marriage or any other kind of serious relationship, despite his obvious maturity. She didn't feel ready.

They leave the bar at dusk to listen to the rappers and their breathtaking recital. People have been drawn to the street corner opposite to hear them speak out against the system and call their brothers to action.

System / worker bro / Kanak bro / they took away / your lands / back then / way back when / and now / land reforms /give your lands / back again / but now / you're a worker / hard labourer / member of the / prolo-/proletariat/mate / em-ploy-ee / in debt / up to your / blue-collar eyeballs / Komrade / Kaledonian / Oceanian / Islanda / sista and brotha / if you got your /own land / got proper / private proper-ty / land own-er / still worker though / hard labourer / prolo- / em-ploy-ee/ in debt / up to your / blue-collar eyeballs / just like me / Kanak worker / shirker / squatter / no land / no dough / livin' high though / show off / opportunist / got a four wheel drive / doin' stunt man / in suburbia / dodging water bills / power bills / stick no bills/ on the/mort-gage man / tax man / get out man / your gears in re-po / good job too / down by law / law's in charge / of every dude / and the masters / of the earth / and all the / owners / and the ex-propriated / thrown off / of their own land / landless / labourers / prolos / layin low / low life / underground / couldn't pay / their own way / land debts / owing land / they don't own / owe it all / to the system / of planetary/ proper-ty / own-ership / Citizens/ men and women / of the flag / I'm a talkin' / to you / red white and blue / boom boom boom / flag the flag / drop her down / let her hang / bang bang bang / things is movin' / bang bang bang / and a shakin' / come with us / out in the streets / march with us / get on yo' feet / here and now / on this square / under the tar / seal road / feel the sand / the earth / the land / Kanak land / Caledonie / Kanaky / tomorrow land / future country / build her togetha / you and me / Caledonie / Kanaky / brothas and

*sistas / mother father / from Kaledonia / Oceania / Islanda / sista
and brotha / all togetha / children / of this country / oh yeah / we
know / past is past / long time passin / passed us by / passed by here
/ what happened to / collective memory / runnin' fast / from the past
/ runnin' on empty / runnin' still / still in us / the past / runnin' past
/ red white an' blue / shoot you down / bang bang / shoot you down
/ bang bang / get down / get back / outta the way / hear what / I say
/ I say no /I say non / non mesdames / non messieurs / no more /
cock and bull / doodledoo / no more past / history / the gall / of our
ancestors / the Gauls / our Kanak ancestors / have jumped / the fence
/ bolted the paddock / of yesterday's / red white an' blue / black and
white / colour barrier / break down / the borders / of this is France /
her colonial past / compassed /and mapped out / and past / out now
/ here and now / here we are / here today / tonight / all togetha now
/ kagou / doodledoo / stand up / stand tall / enfants / de la patrie
/ children of this country / Kanak / Kaledo / Oceanian / Islanda /
homeland / hand in hand / all togetha now / walkin' into / the future
/ we got to build / this country / togetha / land of / tomorrow / citizen
sistas / and brothas / of Kanaky / New Caledonia.*

Another couple of drinks in another couple of bars overflowing
with drunken crowds and they're ready to move on. Early in the
evening, Tom and Léna walk the young cousin back to the barracks.
At the entrance, they bump into their storyteller friend with another
group, also walking a soldier back. She rushes up and kisses Tom on
both cheeks, saying how happy she is to see him again – cos she's just
arrived back in town from her tribe, she explains. And all three put
it down to the booze as they watch her stumble off with her mates,
tottering along in a tight dress and high-heels that click-clack on the
asphalt seemingly in time to her voice as she waves her scarf and
shouts out to anyone who cares to listen:

— *Oyez, oyez, good citizens! Listen up, folks! This is the story of a
fisherman hooked on hooking a huge fish...*

— Get you! Didn't know you had such a flash vocabulary! Word-play an' all!

— So what? Why shouldn't I? You're not the only ones! I been to school too! And that's how come I play with words like you say! But anyway, now you listen to my story and shut up interrupting or else all of youse'll get my fist in your faces! Geddit? So, it's a story about a fisherman...

And the rest of the story is lost in the general laughter she sets off among the group that disappears into the night.

On the way back, laughing like the excited children they had seen in the streets that morning, Tom and Léna run hand-in-hand down the tarsealed slope of the little alley beside the old barracks. When they're almost at the bottom, they catch sight of the waves breaking below them on the shore of the bay, glistening in the lamplight. She thinks she sees a canoe floating past, with someone on board. He can't see a thing and suggests they go and take a closer look. So they walk down the short flight of steps that leads to the water's edge and, there, they forget all about the supposed boat and stand transfixed by the multitude of constellations and the silvery trail of a shooting star that defies the neon lights of the town. There follows a palpable silence that propels them suddenly towards each other.

Chapter 2 – The fisherman

Tom and Léna give in easily to the force that carries them away, yielding to the violent urgency that overwhelms them on the last step down to the sea, as if to obliterate the past. The march, the day out with all its noisy festivity, all those close to them – comrades-in-arms, relations, friends, girlfriends, boyfriends, their mates – disappear, vanish behind them like a lost city sinking beneath the waves. They walk along the seashore looking for a place to themselves on this beach that Tom knows so well because he's launched from here with friends on many a memorable fishing trip. They first settle down on Léna's black and white keffiyeh shawl, behind the peeling, capsized hull of a large wooden boat that has grass growing up all around it and looks like it has been there forever.

The first waves of the rising tide flow gently around the tips of coral, lapping lightly against the rounded shapes of emerging rocks and just beginning to wet the stones along the beach. They mark their passage with little traces of salty foam, before sinking silently into the porous sand. They withdraw lithely, leaving behind grains of sand saturated with salt water, like blotches burned by the sea on skin, only to return the stronger, full of salty zeal, spraying the beach with their seaweed smells. In a silent, secret understanding of their own, they ceaselessly deposit fine beige- and orange-coloured shells, tiny porcelain cowries with their grainy or varnished surfaces and little mauve or violet cones; leaving them in homage, like gifts in return for unnamed favours, or laying them gently along the curves of the reclining beach. With an inaudible whisper, the waves softly finger the blackness of rounded seeds and *bancoule* nuts, like ceremonial pearls or the mourning beads adorning the foreheads, necks and wrists of the dancer in a trance. Other, noisier waves follow, breathing heavy with the surging tide, sighing and smiling and offering up their harvest of kelp, fragile sea urchin shells or broken fingers of coral. Tossed around by the force of the tide, they rush in to dispense their aquatic wasp stings, their frantic, barbed jellyfish bites. Then, under the thrust of the mounting swell and with the impetus of its intense, undulating mass, they end up, as ever, breaking in a tumultuous mass of foam; with one violent shudder surrendering their seminal offerings to the earth. Among two mangrove fruits, a coconut husk and a few bits of driftwood, Tom and Léna lie spent on the sand, motionless like the exhausted wreck, cast up by the sea.

Later, a cool pre-dawn breeze wakes them and they move to the other side of the wreck where they find a large hole, crawl in and take refuge under the upturned hull, now a providential shelter. Deaf to the noise of cars going to the market and boats heading out to sea, they fall straight back to sleep. Oblivious to the voices of kids running to the only shop in the area, to the singing of inebriated soldiers happily making their way back to barracks, or the cries of seagulls flying over the bay, they sleep peacefully, like two babes left behind on the floor of a frail craft in a shipwreck, overcome by the long hours of the previous day and night. Perhaps the mingled odours of oil and sea in the sheltering half-light act on them like an anaesthetic, protecting them against the city that is just waking from the excesses of the day before and the usual Saturday-night fever, to the sound of the cathedral bells. They do not hear the dog barking behind the rusty iron railings and brightly coloured bougainvilleas surrounding a villa on the other side of the road that runs along the beachfront. Nor do they hear the screech of tyres from a black car with two men inside, whose driver slams on the brakes after hurtling downhill from the barracks, as if he has reached a destination. They see nothing of the comings and goings of the various faithful, to and from the Protestant temple or the Catholic cathedral, the fitness fanatics out running or walking, tourists taking photos of the bay before jumping on a bus or back onboard ship. The colours, tones and nuances of the sky beyond the rare cloud appear, pass over and fade away in the morning sun that glides gently over them. An old wino, a regular around the place, sensing an unfamiliar presence on his territory, bends over the opening in the upturned wreck and is moved as he sees them sleeping like babes in the wood. Catching sight of Léna's right hand framing the black rosette with the red heart pinned to her left lapel, he shivers and hurries off, making the sign of the cross and muttering sadly, 'Two more lost kids! What a tragedy! What's the world coming to! Holy Mary, Mother of God, pray for us!'

Around ten, Tom bangs his head against the wall of the wreck and wakes with a start to see Léna tossing and turning, visibly distressed, before opening her eyes. Reassured by his presence, she tells him that she has just been jolted out of a nightmare in which she could see the red and black rosette floating along on the waves, while she herself was drowning in the disturbing shadow of a figure that had been observing them through the hole in the wreck. He pulls her back against him to comfort her and they sail away again to the rhythm of the tides.

In order to preserve a little of their newfound intimacy, Tom goes off alone to get provisions for the day from the old corner shop. He takes the time to reflect on Léna's tumultuous entry into his carefree bachelor existence. For, in fact, it's the very first time that he hasn't felt like taking off the morning after this sort of night; a night when he had found himself incapable of controlling his senses or his feelings, or anything about the force now carrying him away into some magical universe to which his whole being abandons itself, momentarily wiping out all thoughts of the past. Just to be with her, body and soul, here and now, under the wreck. Nothing else. And he surrenders willingly to this state of grace that erases the void he had previously existed in; he's only now realising the extent of its shallow superficiality. He accepts this transfigured state all the more easily because this night spent under the wreck has shown him another self, his double, which had been lying dormant within him. His past is already far, far behind him. And so when he meets a few acquaintances along the way, he greets them absent-mindedly. When one of the girls teases him about the dark circles under his eyes, he merely smiles. He hears laughter coming from behind the shop and recognises the storyteller friend, sitting there looking somewhat dishevelled under the mango tree, waving her scarf to get the attention of her small early-morning audience who are only half awake after their sleepless night.

— The pine trees, the coconut palms, all the trees throughout the entire land were moving like this during the big cyclone. Come on, listen up, you, 'stead of sleeping! It's daytime already! You know it is! Look out there in front of you, the sea, our Pacific Ocean under God's heaven, our Holy Father waiting for you at the Sunday service or at mass for your Sunday morning prayers. Yes, that's what I said, your prayer to the God of the entire universe to wash away your sins of last night. What? Gin already got you knocked out before mass? Well, come on into my cyclone story: it'll wake you all up and take you far, far, far, so far away from here to a land of wonders. Yeah, wonders, like the Seven Wonders of the World. The library of Alexandria, the Egyptian pyramids, the hanging gardens of Babylon. Waa... The Twin Towers... Ja Rastafari. What are the other ones? What're the other Wonders of the World, you lot? Come on; help a girl out here, goddammit! It's full daylight, c'mon, wakey wakey now!

— Oh shut up, Lila in Wonderland! You've already kept us out of our minds all night with your bloody stories. Let us get some sleep now for chrissake!

24

— Sleep? Whad'ya wanna sleep for? Can't you see it's daytime? What's with all this sleeping? You guys do nothing *but* sleep! *Fais dodo, Colin, mon petit frère... Hush little baby, don't say a word, Mama's gonna buy you a mockingbird...* From Lila in Wonderland! *Au clair de la lune, mon ami Pierrot... .*

Walking into the store, Tom doesn't catch the rest of the lullabies that the storyteller chants to calm down the stroppier members of her audience. 'Nan, a customer', says a quavering voice from out of the half shadows lit up by the daylight. The voice belongs to an old man whose hunched shoulders are bent over his account books, nothing escaping the hawk eyes encircled by silver-rimmed glasses. Like a female double, as old as both her male companion and their store, the woman appears behind the counter, a welcoming smile on her lined face. Reigning over the shop is a portrait of a lady, almost spilling out of her stately olden-day frame, wearing a bonnet, a Charleston dress and fancy heeled shoes, Louis XV-style, and carrying a parasol, still offering customers her charming Roaring Twenties smile. Along the rest of the wall, old pictures portray maritime history, from the Roman galley to the steamship, via the caravel and the warship. Below them, on a shelf, like a treasure in its glass case, a miniature sailing ship sits in state beside an outrigger canoe of the same size, made of varnished wood. Vestiges of another era, these cherished objects reveal a little piece of the old couple's past.

The man is son and heir to one of the grand old colonial families and, in his time, went to the naval school for officers. He was one of a long line of ship's captains in his family's distant country of origin; his father, himself a captain in the merchant navy, had sent him there to carry on the family tradition. He had lived in this sailors' world since childhood and was a brilliant student, so had no difficulty following the path that had been laid out for him – while his father, the captain, went on sailing from one island and one mistress to the next. The captain was a charming braggart who made children everywhere he went, as if they were eggs deposited in the belly of each of his women in his 'havens of peace', as he used to call his favourite ports of call.

In his home port he lived several lives, behind the bourgeois façade of respectable colonial society that was at the same time the brunt of his jokes and his greatest source of pride. Things went on like this for years until, one day, he ended up bringing his latest conquest, who could have been his daughter, back home with him. Unable to bear the scandal, his wife, the woman in the picture with the charming smile, left him.

The day his son returned he found the house empty, except for his father's young mistress – the captain having gone back to sea. His mother had informed him of the situation, and the thought of the young woman moving into the family home and taking pride of place had made him decide to direct none but his iciest glare and cruellest remarks towards her. But then, when he first saw her at the gate and was struck by the proud manner in which she carried herself, he knew this vision would remain with him for the rest of his life. And so, when they found themselves face to face, he was as lost for words as she was. He hurriedly deposited his bags in his room and went out, crawling from bar to bar until very late at night. When he got back home, she was sitting in the drawing room with a cup of herbal tea. Reaching out for her hand, he took her in his arms then pulled her to the floor.

As for the wife, presented with the fait accompli of the mistress's presence, and now in full knowledge of her husband's womanising ways, she began to plot her revenge, keeping her eyes and ears open to the gossip in the small, insular, colonial community. Convinced she could see some strange family resemblance between her husband and his mistress, she and her close friends spread the rumour that the young woman was the child of one of his distant concubines. Of course the colony laughed up its sleeve at such a deliciously scandalous rumour. And when they heard about the fatal liaison between the son and the mistress, one by one the friends of the disgraced husband began to desert his house. And the last to find out, by means of an anonymous letter, was the captain, who landed one fine day and walked in off his boat to catch them on the kitchen floor. Without saying a word he went slowly to his study, where he shot himself in the head. Now that she had been avenged, the mother gave the shop by the beach to the young couple to manage in her stead, while she withdrew to her parents' estate in the bush and stayed there, permanently out of reach of scandal.

The old lady serves Tom bread, pâté and mineral water, wondering all the while who he reminds her of – some close friend or relation or an acquaintance she must have lost touch with years ago. And since she can't remember the name, with the natural authority the elderly assume over the young, she asks him where he comes from and what he's doing around these parts. Out of politeness, he replies that he is a fisherman from the Loyalty Islands and that he is getting provisions for the rest of the day, which he will be spending at sea. She congratulates him on his line of work and then starts to complain about Lila and her gang, who spend all their time laughing and shouting, drinking or snoozing under the mango tree out the back, owing her a small fortune, mind you. 'Don't let them have anything more on credit,' Tom says decisively to cut short the tirade.

— But my dear boy, what else can we do when they turn up here drunk all the time, and every time we get the same story: 'Well then, you two old settlers in Kanaky, how's biz-ness? Making plenty? We know you're always good for a wee bottle, a few rollies, bit of a snack, bit of a feed for a bunch of homeless street kids like us. That's our old nan and pop; you're the only ones in this bloody mother of a white town who'll give credit to poor lil' Kanaks like us. In't that right, Nanny? In't it, Pop? Go on then, just this once, one last time!' And every time, it's the last time and every time, it's never the last time!

— Last time for what, Nanny? comes Lila's wine-soaked voice from behind them. 'Well, well, whad'ya know, an old acquaintance! And what might the handsome Tom be doing around here?' she enquires.

— Just a bit of shopping.

— Just a bit of shopping! Nothing else, eh! So what happened to the girl, your soldier cousin's girlfriend, after you walked him back to the barracks last night? Vanished into thin air or into the arms of hunky Tom who must have her hidden away somewhere around here. Listen bro, don't think you can put one across an ol' pro like me. Think I didn't see you eating her up with your eyes yesterday? Well, say something for chrissakes, otherwise I'll think I've hit the bulls-eye, this ol' Lila the flower that smells so strong I give you a headache! That's it, isn't it? Put my foot right in it, this ol' Lila.

Without waiting to hear more, Tom is off, doubly determined to protect his new relationship from all the snake-tongued gossipmongers of the earth. So Lila puts her case to the old shopkeeper.

— You see that, Nanny. I'm telling you! He's running back to that little witch he pinched off his cousin last night. Can you tell me, Nan, I know you and Pop have been stuck together like glue since you were really young, so tell me how come there are sluts like her that go from one cousin to the other, or from father to son? An old lady like you, you've been around, surely you can tell me why. Why, Nanny, why? Why? Why? she says, over and over, suddenly sobbing.

— Come now, Lila, calm down, a big girl like you; big girls don't cry. Come on now!

— But me too, Nanny. I'm just as bad. Stinking trash like all the rest. I've been from one brother to the next. And they were both my uncles. No, Nanny, actually it was my father and his brother, my uncle, that used to take turns raping me, for years and years. A thousand years of pain and shame for me, Nanny. For a thousand years, I died a thousand deaths every night. An eternity of suffering and humiliation that turned my body of pain and my grieving heart to stone. Oh I turned into a heart of stone, Nanny. Yes, a heart of stone in a human body lost and adrift for life. A wreck, nanny. Adrift. A drifting wreck. That's me. That's Lila, big-mouth slut, blabbing off her stories everywhere to hide her shame. Yes, Nanny, I'm no better than the others. I'm worse than the others. But you, Nanny, you love me just the same, you always give me credit. And I thank you for that, Nanny. I thank both of you, you and Pop. Without the two of you, many a time I could've starved to death. Thanks, Nan, thanks Pop. Now I'm

28

gonna go off somewhere and kill myself, me, Lila, the flower that smells so strong I give people a headache!

Pushing herself up from the counter she had been gripping as she emptied out her pain and exorcised her old demons, Lila stumbles for the door, while the old man, still bent over his books, points to his mobile phone to let his partner know he has just called the cops. A bit further on down the road, Tom sees the police van go past and turns around to watch them round up the group of young people still out to it under the mango tree. Not Lila, though. He sees her wander off, a frail silhouette in the morning sun, in the direction of the port where a big ship has just tied up. 'Guess she'll spend the night there. Same ol', same ol'...' thinks Tom. Just then, a black car drives slowly past and he hears the passenger shout out to the driver over the stereo that's thumping out a reggae song, 'Yes she will. I tell you, she told me she'd be around here!' They must've been drinking all night, he says to himself, thinking of the little black rosette with the red heart that he had given Léna, because he has just noticed the same one stuck under the right front wiper of the car.

As for Léna, she's also been turning things over in her mind. For she too is experiencing the same strange plenitude, making her lose her sense of reality and notion of time. She feels utterly disorientated by this sudden passion, devoured by the dizzy sensuality of it, overwhelmed by what is happening and not quite sure where she is. But, unlike Tom, she tries to deny the amazing state of grace that has taken hold of her. And she wonders how to cope with all this happiness, this state of perfect wellbeing radiating from them both, from him and her, as if coming from everywhere and nowhere. Not really understanding what's going on, she concentrates on the most basic and down-to-earth questions to do with the here and now of this Sunday, like, 'Wonder what Tom'll bring back from the shop? How and where will I spend the rest of the day? Wonder if we'll sleep together under the wreck again tonight? Where will my cousins think I am? And what about my ex? Will he go round to pick me up for our Sunday afternoon movie?' So many questions without answers that, instead of providing an escape route, pull her ever more tightly into a vicious circle! So next, she tries to unravel the nightmare she had that morning with the red and black rosette bobbing along on the waves while she was drowning; attempting to convince herself that the dream means she is about to land herself in hot water. She wants to make herself believe she might be walking into a dead end, one she can get out of simply by getting out from under the wreck, right now. But she also wants Tom to come back; and at that moment she sees him approaching. There's no mistaking his silhouette, returning to her against the blinding light of the midday sun. A dog barking from behind the bougainvilleas causes her to look over in that direction and she sees him, the other one, her 'ex' from the previous night, passing by on his way back from the barracks. She knows he's coming to pick her up for the movie. Indifferent to the cries of the seagulls, to the smells of the sea, he's walking quickly so he'll be on time for their date. Giving in to a kind of irrepressible, unspeakable curiosity, even stronger than her desire to hide from him, she savours the meeting of the two men and their brief, inaudible exchange.

Léna is calm and smiling when Tom arrives, and he barely frowns when she nods towards the cousin's retreating form and asks,

— He's gone to pick me up for the movie?

— Yes.

— What did you tell him?

— Nothing. I could hardly tell him you spent the night with me and that you were waiting for me here under this wreck, could I?

He utters these last words with the most natural smile in the world. But Léna is confused and embarrassed by the absurdity of her question and she shrinks back into the shadow of the wreck, pretending to cover her head with her keffiyeh to hide the shame and remorse that come creeping in as she remembers Tom's hot, husky voice in the night, intensifying their pleasure by imagining his cousin spotting them from his watchtower on guard duty. But her ambivalence is no match for Tom's cheerfulness and ardent energy as he devours his pâté sandwich, encouraging her too to eat up, and worry later. Since last night's storytelling session in the café, he can detect the slightest hint of joy, anger or distress on her face, and he can see she's just as anxious as she was after the drowning nightmare. He tells her not to worry about it too much, he'll explain everything to his young cousin later on. Then he eats and drinks, as if to absorb any remaining apprehension or doubt she might still have. He gets her to lighten up, to feel free as a bird, free of the weight of her daily life. Happier than ever before, he laughs, hums, sings, jokes with her, so as to prolong the euphoria of the night. 'I bet you didn't miss a thing just before. I knew you were watching us. I could feel you looking. I'm right, aren't I? Don't you know curiosity killed the cat? Eh?' He says, tickling her. 'And you're a little liar. You didn't give much away there, eh,' she responds. 'Neither did you, yesterday, you didn't give anything away at all... till the evening,' he adds, subjecting her to his quickening pace.

The idea of being caught out by the cousin, there under the wreck, excites them both even more. They don't see the old wino go past, chuckling to himself at their dialogue that breaks off into sighs and orgasmic moans, then sitting down in the shade to eat his bread and wash it down with swigs of red wine. Hearing an ambulance siren over towards the port, he remembers that the old shopkeeper told him a young woman had drowned earlier this morning, and he crosses himself.

Later, while Léna is dressing, Tom goes over to the old man, whom he addresses as grandfather, out of respect for his age.

— So, young fulla, was it good?

— Oh yes. Very good with her. She's my woman.

— I don't need to know the details, son. A woman is a woman. A man's a man. And I'm not sure you can say 'my woman' like you can say 'my bed', 'my house' or 'my car'. What do you think, young fulla?

— Sorry, Grandfather. I spoke without thinking.

— You said it.

— You're right, of course. Who can tell what the future has in store for us?

— I'd say you really don't know her at all.

31

— I found her yesterday.

— If you knew her, maybe you wouldn't be with her.

— Why? Do you know her, Grandfather?

— Like she was my own daughter.

— So you really do know her then?

— This is a small country, son, so you guess a lot of things, you know a lot of people.

— You know me too, Grandfather?

— Like you were my own son.

And he names their respective parents as old acquaintances, to the considerable surprise of Léna, who arrives just in time to hear him vaguely recall an afternoon spent with her and her parents, when she was still a little girl, by the wreck of the canoe, down by the sea.

When Tom asks him about his identity, the old man answers by telling the spellbinding story of his chaotic childhood, in the absence of his parents who had left to go from tribe to tribe, carrying out their pastoral mission. Becoming the protégé of his widowed grandfather and the spoiled favourite of the extended family due to his quasi-orphaned status, he quickly learned the ins and outs of custom from the speeches of the elders; and the ins and outs of life from the swearwords that peppered the everyday language of the old women. Very early, he went on to learn the games of love, encouraged by his grandfather, who was not above a few such games himself, despite his age. He used to say that there was nothing like young flesh to make an old ogre's mouth water, like in the stories. He told him that the ogres and ogresses of fairytales, in cannibalistic societies, were none other than cannibal hunters and their women. And he was a direct descendant of cannibals, since his own father had been one, in his day. What's more, he had never been christened and so was not bound by Christian principles, for which he didn't give a damn. And so, caught between his parents' biblical verses, his grandfather's pagan speeches and enjoying secret pleasures of the flesh with his grandfather's women, he had no difficulty choosing sides. He went with his grandfather and his women.

He and his grandfather slept in the old man's thatched house, on mats spread out on top of dried straw around the central fireplace. He and the women would bring in big pieces of dry wood to keep the fire going. And in the evenings, while the women were busy in the cookhouse, he would listen to his grandfather's teachings as he watched the first flames rising from the dried coconut leaves that gave off a delicious burning smell. He would take one from the fire to light his ancestor's pipe, or the cigarettes he made from stray bits of tobacco rolled in a tiny rectangle of dried banana leaf that added a very distinctive flavour. He would listen for hours as his grandfather taught him about his culture, his values, his traditions; his coughing punctuating the lessons by the firelight. The women would bring them pieces of cooked yam or taro on plates made of woven coconut palm leaves, or set down beside them a few *kumwala* and *warei*[6] cooked in embers and some salted or smoked fish on a seared green banana leaf. They would leave the men for a long while to eat and talk, before clearing away the leftovers and withdrawing to the women's house. He discovered later that some of them would return to honour their husband in another way. He would hear them whispering and moaning in the dark, gasping for breath as if they had just climbed to the top of a high mountain. Sometimes, he would manage to make out their entwined, moving bodies as an ember flared. And then, one night, a hand lost its way and found his body and he played along as if he had been waiting for just that. After that, he was pampered by the women; he soon became as adept as they were, and could get anything he wanted from them.

And so it continued until the day his grandfather decided he should have his own house and lead the life of an adult, having undergone all the rites of passage from early childhood to puberty, and finally the rites that marked the end of adolescence. He went up with the men into the forest to choose the wood and the vines, while the women cut the straw and wove the coconut fronds. His maternal uncles took charge of the building of his house, and, when it was finished, they welcomed him into it with his grandfather, their clan and allies, to

6   *Paicî* terms for sweet potatoes and root vegetables. (Transl.)

33

seal his marriage to one of their daughters. He submitted without protest to the matrimonial arrangements of the elders; after all, he had had plenty of time to submit the girl to his every desire, many a time, on the black rock of the wreck of the first ancestral canoe. He used her as he wished, between trysts with his initiatory mistresses from when he lived at his grandfather's house, and it was they who delivered the young women's three children, until the last birth cost her her life. One of the mistresses soon replaced her as the young man's companion and brought up his children. They lived together until the death of the ancestor, who was said to have been the sacrificial victim of the maternal uncles, who were taking revenge for the affront to their daughter and their lineage. He was forced to flee their wrath after an affair that ended in the death of a young girl, and after he had taken a mistress who had barely reached puberty. And this is how he came to be washed up here in the city, with his young mistress, living in his hut near the wreck. She would leave him one night, years later, with a very young man who would have been Tom's age and who looked so like him, they could've been brothers.

As for the wreck, it used to be called the *Coral Rose*, which, as its owner herself told him at the time she was having all that trouble with her husband, was the name given her by her indigenous nanny. Her tenacious personality had been forged by a childhood and youth spent in the bush where, at a very young age, her nanny had shown her how to work the fields and taught her about the harsh realities of that existence. She always longed to go back there, even during the most prosperous days of her life in the town where Coral Rose and her nanny had been forced to follow her husband. When she was fifteen, she had fallen madly in love with a sea captain – her future adored husband – when she saw him disembark from the longboat and stride along the quay, discussing coffee prices with her father, the wealthiest settler in the area. He, for his part, ignored her – until dinner, when she was seated opposite him and when she suddenly felt the rounded tip of his exploring right boot gently nudge against her belly. Fascinated by this somewhat unexpected invitation, she later went to his room, where he made her his slave.

34

He succeeded in convincing her parents that civilised city life would offer the same benefits as a convent finishing school to a young girl of her social standing. In this way he tore her away from them; she was followed by her nanny, then around thirty years of age. The very next day, during a brief stop in a bay, he said he wanted to show them some crabs in the nearby mangroves. Once there, he ordered them to daub each other's bodies with mud, then do the same to him, and then he obtained everything he wanted from each of them.

On the next leg of the journey, he took them to a stable to watch the little 'bayou', as he called the daughter of the local Javanese tenant farmers, while she milked the cows. He pretended to do the same to all three before laying each one on the earthen floor, littered with cow dung and straw. And thus he subjected them to his will, at every step of the journey of the long years he spent with the two of them and all the others, some of whom bore more children to swell the numbers of his descendants. Like the nanny, who disappeared long enough to give birth to one of the natural sons of the adored husband. Of course, his Coral Rose knew nothing of it, as long as she lived.

Coral Rose. Her nanny had given her this name in order to convince her that she was a beautiful coral flower who, like a siren, charmed all sailors – but first and foremost the handsome captain who had chosen her from among all those others to be his wedded wife. To put up with it all, she had had the strength of those little bits of white coral that lie along the beach and somehow resist being crushed underfoot. And alone among them all, she had skin that was as immaculately white as coral washed up by the same sea that will periodically carry off, far away from them both, the seafaring husband and the mud and the dung and the sludge and the slime of his male fantasies. With leaves and stalks and bark medicines, the nanny would bandage her charge's bruises and soothe her black eyes and her swollen, bashed belly. She made sure that her Coral Rose had only one child, a son, so that 'she would not give off the raw flesh smell of childbirth'. When her mistress asked her what she meant by this, she would invariably reply, 'So that you don't smell of fish, as people say.' And so the nanny fussed over her like this all her life, her Coral Rose, trodden under the seafaring foot of the unfaithful handsome captain, a captive slave under his philandering boot.

The old fisherman told Tom he had learnt all this from Coral Rose herself, and that he too, in his time, had been *her* slave, subjected to all the depravities she could imagine, so she could take revenge on her husband, blow for blow. Sometimes even on the *Coral Rose*, when she was still a fine boat, on stormy, full-moon nights, she would beg him to whip her unrepentant nymphomaniac body till it could take no more. 'And today, Coral Rose still smiles at us from her frame over in the old store,' he concludes. Then he asks Tom, as if it were urgent,

— Have you heard the news?

— What news?

— You were with her yesterday, weren't you?

— With who, Grandfather? Who?

— Lila.

— Yes, yesterday morning. We saw her again in a bar yesterday afternoon. And we bumped into her again last night, in front of the barracks.

— Poor wee thing! Holy Mary, Mother of God, pray for us! Holy Mary, Mother of God, pray for her! And may she rest in peace now, with all the Saints in Heaven!

— Who are you talking about, Grandfather?

— The girl who drowned. May God rest her soul!

— What girl?

— Lila.

— No, it can't be her! I saw her again at the store, just this morning. She talked to me, even.

— Death has a will of its own.

— But Grandfather, I saw her this morning, I did!

— And death does have a will of its own.

— Maybe it's some other girl. But not Lila.

— It was Lila who drowned in the harbour this morning.

— You saw her, Grandfather?

36

— May as well have.

— So, it's still possible it wasn't her.

— You've got to believe me, son. The girl who died was Lila.

— Then we have to go to the morgue.

— In any case, they'll soon get the two that murdered her.

— Who are you talking about, Grandfather?

— The two guys who came here looking for her this morning.

— Did you speak to them?

— No. I just told them I didn't know any Lila, except the flower that smells so strong it gives you a headache. And before they drove off, the driver shouted threats at me, 'You old dickhead! Dirty old dog! You better watch your back, we're gonna get you too, one of these days. Gottit, fleabag? Go on back to your scrounging, go on back to your rubbish bins, get you a feed, you dirty old piece of shit!' and all the time pointing, jabbing his finger at me like this. And when the cops came past afterwards, I gave them a description of them and their black car with the number plate, the little black blossom with the red heart on it under the right front wiper, the lot. That'll teach 'em. I may be an old piece of shit but they are sure as anything gonna be sleeping inside tonight, and for a long time, believe you me! And me, I was born free as the wind and free I'll stay, as long as I live.

— Right, I know who you mean, Grandfather! Those two guys you're talking about passed me in their black car on my way back from the shop this morning. It's true they were looking for her because they were driving really slowly and I heard the passenger yell out to the driver, 'Yes she will. I'm telling you, she told me she'd be here!'

— So they're done for, son. Believe me, old Tom says so. And when old Tom says something's gonna happen, it happens. Every time, without fail. They'll be sleeping inside tonight, or my name's not old Tom. Old piece of shit, free as the wind, Tom! See you later then, kids, enjoy your Sunday, both of you! Death passes by and life goes on.

Tom and Léna go off and spend the afternoon a bit further along the beach, behind a big rock where the remains of a bonfire is

37

evidence of the popularity of the spot. As are all the graffiti messages, signed, dated, anonymous or in code, carved onto the leaves of an aloe bush; they have great fun reading them. The plant is a veritable visitor's book, where the entries go from the humorous to the fanciful – sometimes in abbreviations, sometimes in numbers, sometimes written in full. And in several languages.

I luv u mon amour for ever. I A door U, signed JVS. T KIRO BLACK MAGIC WOMAN sed SANTANA ABRAXAS. Amour rhymes with Toujours. It's now or never. PLIZ NVR FRGT ME. I love you forever. Aou ka!⁷ Doan let me down. Where did my lovey dovey go? The bird's flown the coop. Cooped up without you. Plenty more fish in the sea. One in every port. Hello sailor. Heart-breaker. Don't forget your jandals. Depends who's who in this live KNKY broadcast. Rmmbr me alwys my darling. Souvenir of 1 naked nite. Go put sth on. WOT? WOTSUP? WOTSWIDUMAN? WOTSETINU? Still luvu, stupid, signed ET. All the same on the planet. The planet's off the pla-net on the net. Hoo sed? Internet's kool. Yeah. Internet's interplanetary luv, cosmik luv. U R my Infinity. ALFA + OMEGA = U. Gotta have u near or far, baby. Because I love you too much baby. Don't hurt me too much, mi amor. Lovesickness iz easy cured. No wham bangers need apply. Gimme a man with a slow hand. All night long, babe. Let me love you like the night compares with U. U and Me, too much. Mega kool. Kool Runnings, that's a film. No film like Terminator. You're terminated. Hasta la vista Baby. It's all over mi amor. Till the end of time, I'll be with you. Till the end. Till death us do part, babe. Near or far. Baby u can drive my car. Doan have no accident though. Aou! Doan say like that! Don't worry baby. I'll always b here. Got the hots for u. Hot summer night hots for u. Hot-blooded hots. Hot blood cools fast. Babe u so cool. 2 B alone with u. At the end of the day. Hell I luv u. Hell and back. Cross my heart. Cure me quick. Yr hot love is burnin me. Kindly extinguish fire when finished or on exiting permanently. Put out yr fags. Throw no butts. Light no fires. Protect our forests! What about moi? Moi

7   Kanak exclamation (Transl.)

38

here, Aloe, you guys are cutting me up! 2 true! No more writing on this here poor plant, OK? OK, your go!

As his con*tribu*tion, Tom simply writes T+L followed by the date.

They spend the afternoon laughing, horsing around and resting. Tom has no trouble coming up with jokes and funny faces and silly imitations that prolong Léna's carefree laughter, so he can go on soaking it up. He gets a kick out of letting her win their swimming and diving races, just to see her pout as she splashes him and says, 'Right, I quit. You're a cheat!' 'What about this then. Is this cheating?' he asks, laughing, after giving her a long, breathtaking kiss, their lips barely above water. And without waiting for her to reply, he does it again and again, until he is floating inside her on the rising tide. After an eternity, exhausted by his frantic and playful lovemaking, she suggests a short siesta in the shade.

Happy as a little kid on holiday, overtaken by his excess of energy, Tom falls asleep immediately. Léna lies awake staring at the horizon, wondering how her cousins could have explained her disappearance the day before to her ex. She's sure he won't insist on seeing her and that he'll probably go off with some of his own cousins or his army mates, like the two young French guys who call them 'the two good little kiddies'. In her mind's eye she can see them in the queue at the ticket office, opposite the drinks counter, waiting to find a row of empty seats so that they can sit together in the dark theatre and be carried away for two hours by the magic of the silver screen. She goes over memories that connect her to her usual routines, to her everyday life as it was until the night before – the life which, perhaps, she is reluctant to leave behind, in spite of all the delicious intensity of the events of the last twenty-four hours. And she has no idea how to explain things to the young soldier, even if he did come across as someone who would understand it all perfectly. But she thinks it's up to her to do it, since she's the one who ended the relationship last night. She's not sure she's brave enough, though, and she also considers running away from it, laying low for a bit till things calm down, rather than having a full-on confrontation right now.

A heron's call interrupts this last thought, and she calls herself a cowardly bitch for thinking it; then she goes back into her past, further back again, and relives her mother's dying moments. For a long while she turns over other guilty memories in her mind, then finally she falls asleep. And wakes a little later, tossing and turning. Terrified.

A nightmare has her frozen to the spot, unable to move or call for help. In it, she sees Lila, every bit as alive as she was yesterday, twisting the aloe leaves around her arms, singing the following words to her, to the tune of a nursery rhyme:

> You are Lola the agave
> Succulent as a love poem
> You turn heads
> As they wait their turn
> You give pleasure
> Messenger goddess of love
> I am Lila sour grapes
> Lila the headache
> They turn their backs
> I make their heads spin
> Till they spin off and die
> I am the messenger of Death.

Then Lila disappears out to sea on a canoe she can't see, with children who laugh at her, taking up the tune in unison as a lullaby. At that moment, a laughing dwarf, with the face of the old hobo fisherman, rips off the aloe leaves one after another and throws them onto the waves, shouting at the top of his voice, 'Make love not war', like a slogan on one of the placards in yesterday's march, then, 'Gone with the wind'. The leaves float around and away like pages torn from a book, disappearing out to sea, and then a big wave comes and throws up, like a shipwreck on the wet sand, the little black rosette with the red heart.

Chapter 3 – Lila

At dusk when they return to the wreck, retracing their steps along the beach, the old fisherman is no longer there. They decide to go and get a few things from the shop – and to get the latest from the old couple on the inquiry into Lila's death. The moment she catches sight of them, the old woman starts talking about their friend.

— There you are, you two, oh my God, I suppose you've heard about poor Lila?

— Yes, but we don't know whether she really drowned herself, says Tom.

— Oh, so you don't know then? No, poor wee thing! That's one thing we know for sure, she didn't drown! She was raped, strangled, then thrown into the sea. May the Lord keep her soul, up there where she is now.

— So who do you reckon did it?

— The two guys who came looking for her this morning.

— Really? So there were two guys looking for her?

— Yes siree! And they were none too sober. In fact, they were well on the way. I'd even hazard a guess they'd had a few puffs as well. No two ways about it, a couple of druggies.

— What'd you say to them?

— Who to? The two guys or the police?

— To the whole lot of them – the whole shooting box.

— Well, to the two guys I said I had no idea who they were looking for. I said 'Lila, Lila, hang on, that's the name of a flower, not a woman's name' – because I didn't like them one bit, those two!

— An' then?

— An' then they started threatening us, shouting, 'Listen, Grandma, flower name or woman's name, that's not your problem. And I hope for your sake you not mucking us around cos if you are, we'll be back, ya know, and we'll pay you a bit of a visit, you and old Gramps over there. And after that, we'll torch this dump. OK? You heard didn't you, Grandpa, what we just told your ol' lady here? See my finger, this one, right, well it'll hurt bad when I stick it up somewhere. So you olds better watch it, right!' And he was sticking out his middle finger, wiggling it around like they always do to threaten you. And, oh my God, the shouting!

— So what did you do?

— Well, nothing, you know, at our age. So, we just waited for them to finish their carry-on and leave. Which they did – but not before pinching two cartons of cigarettes and two casks of wine. And the one that did the talking shouted at us again, 'This is for our breakfast. And if we're still hungry, later on, we'll be back and help ourselves to some more, OK? And no funny business, right, fossils, otherwise we'll do your place over. OK! Right, hasta la vista, old fossils!'

— Jeez. They sound pretty scary!

— You bet! Couple of hoods! Real gangsters, just like on the telly! So, just after they got back in their car, Pop called the police on his mobile and gave them their description and the numberplate, and told them all about the threats and everything they stole from us and all. Oh yes, and there was this little black and red paper flower stuck under the right front wiper. Because they were parked just outside the window, over there, so Pop could write it all down neat and proper for the police.

— And how did things go after that?

43

— Well, all that business started just after you went back over to the beach, down by the wreck. Surely you must've seen them?

— Yes. I saw them go past.

— Well, there you are. You saw what they looked like. Those two sure weren't joking. Real scary, they were! Like they were old hands at it – stealing and threatening people and all the rest. Oh là là! Look at that, I've still got goose bumps! So, where was I? You go off down to the wreck and Lila, poor darling, she comes back in and tells me all about the terrible things she went through at home, then she thanks us both, in tears, me and Pop, thanks us for giving her credit, then she says 'adieu' – that she's going off somewhere to kill herself! Some suicide! More like a rape and murder, I'd say! Those two murderers took turns at raping her then they strangled her! They're damn lucky they did away with the guillotine! Dear God, they've got to be punished, because you know, Lila was a good girl – always paid back what she owed us. Late sometimes, but she always paid her debts. She was a good girl in that way. And that's why they've got to pay for their crime, those two criminals! Please, dear God, see that justice is done for our poor little Lila!

— They must've caught up with her further down the road, cos I know I saw her walking off towards the port before I went back to the wreck.

— Yes, they caught her, took her down into the mimosas, raped her first and strangled her afterwards. Then, they threw her body into the water so it would look like she drowned.

— That's what the cops said?

— Yes, they told us. Because, just between ourselves, whatever goes on around the neighbourhood, Pop always keeps them informed, so it's only natural they return the favour now and again, eh?

— So did they find the two guys?

— Yes, they got 'em. Arrested and taken over the other side, over to the Far West[8] and locked up, late this afternoon. They were at a

---

8 *Far West* is the English nickname for the *Camp Est* or *East Camp*, the territorial prison. (Transl.)

mate's place, those two murderers, sleeping peacefully if you please. Of course, with everything Pop told the cops when he dobbed them in, it didn't take them five minutes to follow up the leads and find them. They even brought back what was left of the cartons of cigarettes they stole from us. Not the wine, of course, that's bound to be what knocked them out, so the cops were able to come in and nab 'em. Anyhow, good on them, I reckon, especially Pop, because, let me tell you, there isn't a better police informer anywhere in this town. And to think some people call him a dirty grass or an old pimp, when he does it for everyone's good! But, there are some really nasty types out there, especially to poor old folks like us. It's downright sickening, that's what it is!

— So all in all, he's the perfect grass. By the way, the cops pay you a bit for it or what?

— That'll be the day! We don't need that at our age. We only do it for the common good and for the good of the business community in our little town. Business is business, as the Pokens[9] say – so there you have it! At any rate, God will see to it we get our just deserts when our time comes, don't you think?

— Just so long as justice is done for Lila.

Pretty well up with the play by now, Tom buys what they need for the evening. On the way back to the wreck they go over their memories of Lila over the last forty-eight hours or so – her words, her stories, everything she did and said. And Léna wonders how their own story will end, beginning as it has with the death of their storyteller friend. And she thinks to herself that Lila really did have the last laugh, with the stories she told them the day before, as if she were thumbing her nose at both life and death, as if the two were one and the same. Or maybe love and death, like in the dream she had had this afternoon. By calling her 'Lola, the agave', Lila was comparing her to the aloes and predicting that

---

9   *Pokens* is a colloquial Caledonian term for English language speakers, particularly Australians and New Zealanders, derived from the expression, "English spoken". (Transl.)

she too would be cut up by those who would love her. Or perhaps it meant that she was destined to live it up, love it up and then die. 'Make love not war.' Anyway, they were all stories written by various destinies, gone with the wind of memory and memories, like pages on the waves of life and on the immense ocean swell of death. 'Gone with the wind,' screamed the dwarf in the nightmare as the pages flew away and the invisible canoe sailed off towards the horizon, and the chorus of Lila and the children laughed at her with their nursery rhyme song. But she doesn't tell Tom anything of this dream, which she sees as yet another bad omen for their relationship, like Lila's death. And when he says he's sure they'll run into the old wino down by the wreck, she shudders, as if he too, like the little black rosette with the red heart, was a premonitory character in their own story.

Sure enough, they see firelight on the beach, just beyond the wreck. And sure enough, Léna gives in and joins Tom and they go over to the fisherman. Catching sight of them, he calls out.

— That you, children? Com 'n' warm yourselves up over here by the fire! We all need a bit of warmth, with all this bad news. And on a Sunday, what's more! You'd think there was no day left to think of our Father in Heaven.

— Have you eaten, Grandfather? Tom enquires. We've got bread, pâté and cheese. There's some fruit juice too, he adds, showing their plastic bags full of food.

— No thanks, son. I've already started on my wine to keep me warm and I'll have a bit more to help me sleep later. Then he breaks into an old French drinking song that goes something like: *I'll have another one, Oui oui oui. Another two, non, non non. Till I've drunk a thousand bottles, oui!* You gotta sing, my children, keep on singing to chase away the blues! *Oui*, never forget to sing!

— We've just come back from the shop. Tom breaks in.

— Yes, I saw you going over that way.

— Did you? We didn't see you at all.

— That's how it is. Now you see me, now you don't.

46

— Why's that, Grandfather? You like playing hide-and-seek or something?

— Ah, always got a joke up your sleeve, eh son! Good thing too, life is so sad sometimes. But tell me, what did those two over in the shop tell you? That old lady over there, especially. Jeez can she talk, eh! Talks and talks so much, you have to stop her sometimes or she'll make your head spin. So what'd she say?

— She said that the two murderers are the guys in the black car from this morning. She says they threatened them and stole some booze and smokes. Yeah, and she said Pop informed the cops, and that they did it down in the mimosas then threw her in the water. And that they were arrested late afternoon.

— Just like I told you this morning, son, just like this free-as-a-bird old bastard of a Tom said!

— You're no bastard, Grandfather. No one's a bastard really. We're all men and women.

— Except for him up there, watching over us from above. I know all that, son. But I still say I'm a bastard among bastards, or a wreck like that one right there beside us. There are the bastards and the wrecks and then there are the others, like you two. There are the murderers and the victims. That's how the world is, son. And there's nothing you can do about it. That's how the Good Lord set it up.

— Yes, but a person can make up for the bad things they've done. A person can change.

— You reckon? It's just like you to say that, son. Yes, a person can make up for things, go to confession, pay their debt to society. But what's done is done. And there's nothing you can do about that. No one can bring Lila back, son. No one! Hear me? That's what I'm trying to get you to understand.

— I know, Grandfather. But what about you, you're not a murderer or a bastard.

— Aren't I? How do you know? What do you know about me? We only met this morning. You know nothing about me. Isn't that true, son?

— We don't need to know.

— That's what you say. We don't need to know. How convenient. That way everybody's happy. Who is who, it's so much better not to know.

— Isn't it better that way, Grandfather?

— It's better for you, but it might be worse for her, he says, nodding towards Léna.

— What's better for me can be better for her too.

— That's where you're wrong, son. Because a thing like that, you can't say because you can't know. It's already hard enough to say what's good or better for one's self, so you can imagine how hard it is for others, your girlfriend or anyone else.

— True, it's not easy if you complicate things.

— Well there's nothing more complex than human beings.

— Maybe they want it that way, eh?

— It's something they can't want. It's outside of their free will.

— Meaning?

— Meaning that here we are, the three of us. Us two are talking. She's not. She's here but she's off in some other place too, she's thinking about her ex, about Lila, or about tomorrow. And that's outside of her free will and outside of your free will and my free will too. Who's ever been able to control thought? No one, so far I as know.

— Some claim they have ways.

— Ways and means, as they say, but they're still looking for more every day, because all their 'ways and means', as they call them, are never good enough.

— So they keep looking and they'll be looking for a long time yet.

— Oh yes, they'll be looking for a long time yet, son. But they'll never have the *mana*, as our Polynesian brothers call it.

— Tell us about *mana*, Grandfather.

— It's the inner force we all have within us.

— Everybody has it within them?

— Everybody has it, but in some people it's asleep and in others it's alive and at work.

— You have to wake it up then?

48

— Depends what for. Because it's not always used for good.

— For example?

— For example, people who use black magic.

— How do they do that?

— They use their *mana* to do evil.

— And what are the leaves and bark and magic packets for?

— Oh, those are just the visible paraphernalia.

— So you don't always need them?

— The ones that really have the power don't need them.

— What's wrong with the ones who do need them?

— Their inner force isn't enough for them.

— And what is this inner force made of?

— Everything that is in you that isn't subject to what's imposed on you from outside.

— But everything's imposed on me. My humanity, my gender, my colour, my family, my social status, my custom, my religion, my country. And heaps of other things.

— Exactly, this force is what can set you free from all that.

— By staying an outsider like you, Grandfather?

— Not necessarily. Power can only be exercised with others.

— But that's not what you chose, is it Grandfather?

— How would you know, son? You know nothing about me, like I just told you.

— Bit hard to believe.

— You'd better believe it, son. I told you that, too, at lunchtime.

— Yes, but it's always hard to believe in invisible powers and occult forces.

— It's only natural, what with the Spanish Inquisition and all.

— What?

— The white man's religion, pastors and priests that did away with all of that.

— Do you think their brainwashing and cleaning-up will have had the desired effect?

— They should've swept in front of their own front door first.

This force I'm talking about can't be erased with a crucifix or a bulldozer. And the Masters of the Inquisition know very well what it's used for.

— So, that kind of power can't be erased?

— No. Not as long as we're still here. As long as there are men. As long as there are women.

Suddenly Léna, who's been sitting close to Tom, slumps forward, face down, very close to the fire. Tom picks her up and runs his hand across her forehead, calling to her,

— Léna! Léna, darling! Come back, darling, come back.

— I'll do it, son! says the fisherman, tapping the young woman lightly on the cheeks.

She comes to, with a suspicious glance at the old man because when she had fainted, she had imagined she was on a canoe that she sensed belonged to the fisherman. That was his true home, somehow.

— There, darling, lay your head on me, suggests Tom, drawing Léna's head down onto his outstretched legs.

— Poor little thing! It's no wonder, with what happened to Lila today. And Lila being at the café with you yesterday when you first met, the stories must've really affected her. These things get to you. But you mustn't think about things too much, child. Chase away the ghosts of the past! Because when they disturb us a bit too much, people end up thinking you're a bit disturbed, if you see what I mean.

— So you were at the café yesterday, Grandfather? How come we never saw you? I would've definitely noticed you.

— Yes, I was there, son, and at the bar, the day one of your conquests made a scene. It's like before, when you came by here and didn't see me. Sometimes you see me. Sometimes you don't. Like I told you before.

— That reminds me of Lila when she used to say that with her ol' man, it was 'now you see me, now you don't', because that was the best way to make love and pleasure last, according to them. Is that true, d'you think, Grandfather?

— That's a question for you young ones, son. I'm too old to answer that one.

— Yeah, but that's just what I mean, you been there, you know enough to teach us a thing or two!

— Yes, but it's not enough to know things. You have to know them really well. And me, well I don't know much about love and sex anymore today, at my age. Sometimes I wonder just how you manage, with all these new diseases, AIDS and drugs and all.

— We're careful, Grandfather, we use condoms.

— And so how do you manage to get children and descendants then?

— Good question, Grandfather! But we get tested to make sure we haven't got anything.

— Yes, but you'll always get the smart-arses who don't let on and pass it on to their partners and they pass it on to others and so on.

— You always have to have condoms on you.
There are women's ones too.

— Women's ones too? Well I didn't know that.

— We do what we have to, to protect ourselves.

— That's good. But it sure doesn't bode well for the future of mankind and womankind on earth.

— It won't be any worse than in the past though?

— Who can tell?

— We'd better hope it won't be.

— Hope keeps you alive and hope kills you.

— Kills you?

— Don't people die, fighting for a better world?

— Yes, but they're always hoping they won't have to die, aren't they?

— No doubt, but dying for an ideal is part of the history of mankind.

— Yes, and so is living for an ideal, and that's just as hard.

— It sure is, son. It's just as hard to live by one's ideas, against everyone, as it is to die for them.

— Dying for ideas! What an idea! Man invents the things he wants to live and die for as well.

— Only when he can afford the luxury. Otherwise he dies – when hunger and poverty won't let him survive. That's why there are so many youth suicides nowadays.

— That's what Lila told the old lady from the shop she was going to do, just before those two guys arrived. 'I'm going off somewhere to kill myself.' Those were her last words.

— Poor child! Holy Mary, Mother of God, have mercy on us, poor sinners! Holy Mary, Mother of God, have mercy on her, poor Lila!

— So you knew her well too, Grandfather?

— Do I know her? You bet, son. I know her family; I watched our little Lila grow up.

— Tell us what you know about her!

— Well, Lila's short for Delilah, the name her father gave her the day she was born. It was the day after he'd seen a film about Samson and Delilah, the strong man in the Bible and his wife who betrayed him by cutting off his hair, the secret of his strength, one night while he was asleep. Actually, her father more or less meant the name to be a revenge against her mother, whom he suspected of cheating on him. He wasn't entirely sure he was the real father of the beautiful baby who was to become our beautiful little black doll that everyone spoiled. She was everyone's pet. Afterwards, she didn't stay at school long, back in the mining centre. She used to run away a lot, and her grandmother came to get her to live with her in the *tribu*. Then her father came to take her back to look after her mother who was sick. Lila cared for her faithfully until she died. After that, she left home to start a life of her own in town, running round with boys, left right and centre. And whenever she ran out of dough, she knew where to find me, in memory of her childhood days. And that's how she ended up living on the street, hanging round here, asking those two oldies in the shop for credit. And there you have it. That's the life story of Lila. Poor little Lila! Holy Mary, Mother of God, have mercy on her! And open up the gates of heaven to her this very evening! God rest her soul!

Feeling like she's going to vomit, Léna gets up and walks down towards the sea. Tom follows her, waving goodbye to the old fisherman, who says, 'Yes, we'd better be getting to bed, the kid's not well at all, with all that's happened to poor Lila! Goodnight and God bless you, children!' When Tom asks her, 'Not feeling too good, babe?' Léna explains that, as the old man was telling them the story of Lila's life, she had felt nausea rising uncontrollably inside her. 'Like the old man says, we're all a bit shaken up by this whole thing. C'mon, my darling, let's get some sleep,' Tom suggests, as he takes her by the hand and leads her down the beach. Hugging him tight, Léna adds, 'Yes, I'll feel better tomorrow,' as if to convince herself she will. He kisses her long and tenderly and hurries her back to the wreck.

But his passion is no longer enough to rid her of this sudden, unexpected revulsion towards the old vagrant. When he speaks, all the ghosts of her past come flooding back in, like this afternoon, twisting the fisherman's words around with malicious glee. She tells Tom she's really sleepy, so that he'll leave her to savour in secret the strangely exalted feeling that grips her, a feeling of searching for things buried somewhere deep within her consciousness. It's like the excitement a detective gets when he senses he's about to uncover the clue that will open the gates of truth. 'Naked, cruel, indecent – whatever. I must have the truth. And I will track it down until it hits me in the face,' Léna says to herself, as she struggles through the labyrinth of tortured thoughts that bring her back again and again to the fisherman, like a missing piece of the puzzle of her life. Sleep overcomes her, but she is jolted out of it by another nightmare, in which Lila and the children start singing the nursery rhyme again, in chorus, in a frenzied *pilou* dance, banging against the side of the wreck as if it were a tam-tam. Stuck to the inside of the hull, the fisherman's face watches her, with a glassy-eyed, lascivious, provocative gaze. Teasing her almost for her powerlessness against the hold he has over her; almost as if she were his sex object, some perverse plaything. She wakes with a start and realises that the dancing in the dream was only the sound of driving rain pounding the wreck. She goes out for a moment then comes back in and shakes Tom, who was sound asleep, to get him to call a taxi. And they go back to his studio apartment.

The night before Lila's funeral, which has been postponed for the police inquiry, family and friends take turns keeping watch over the body in one of the air-conditioned rooms at the morgue. Tom and Léna, too, bring along their lengths of fabric for the customary offering, together with a bunch of red anthuriums[10]. It's a little private joke in reference to her story about the taro collector.

The icy peacefulness of death has fixed Lila's features in a serenity outside the time of the living and its attendant horrors. Its violations and its violence. Its unpunished crimes. Children violated, women victims of violence. Unpunished crimes perpetrated by carpet salesmen, arms dealers and dream merchants who use and abuse the female body like some fine filly or some brood mare up for sale in classifieds, commercials and on billboards on every street corner – outdoing each other in degrading womanhood, bringing her down to the status of beautiful sexual commodity. Sexy at all cost and at any price. Even if the price to pay is parity, if need be, since one doesn't preclude the other. And Lila has been murdered, like so many other sisters before and after her, to keep her in her designated place as the whore who dared touch a single hair on the head of the he-man with his murdering rapist's sex and his criminal strangler's hands. Jack the Ripper ain't dead. Even in a little Pacific town, on the other side of the world from the back streets of Mister Hyde's Soho. And further up, to the north by northwest, Mister Butchery carves up Iraqi and Afghan civilians and farmers at the mercy of his bombs. Mister Bullshit. Big names waiting for political parity and all the Delilahs who might still dare to threaten the virility of the Samsons, on the threshold of the third millennium after the sweet Lord Jesus. It's scarcely credible! And yet, Lila is there all right, lying on her back with a final mocking half-smile, thumbing her nose at death, wearing a glittering party dress and a red scarf round her neck to cover the marks where she was strangled.

---

10 The *anthurium* is a tropical genus with spectacular, large, heart-shaped flowers, impressive, phallic pistils and leaves that are reminiscent of taro. (Transl.)

And Tom remembered the first time he met Lila, not long after he came back from the army, one evening, in a little *nakamal*[11] down by the mangrove, where he and his mates and girlfriends sometimes went for a few shells.[12] He heard Lila encouraging a young activist who was there selling the party rag.

'It's good what you're doing, sista, and I'm with you heart and soul. We may be a bunch of no-hopers, homeless squatters and riff-raff and whatever else they call us. But don't think we don't see what you're doing for us and for everyone in this country, Kanaky. Yeah, you heard me. I said for everyone in this here country of ours. Cos we've taken a few hits for the cause, with all the brothers that've gone down all over, on the land of our ancestors, in our country, Kanaky.

'And today, and you gotta remind 'em, sista, all those short memory assholes running round the place, everybody's getting something, everybody's cashing in on the ADN,[13] godammit! Pardon the language, sis, but I'm not talking about the DNA the scientists are on about but about our *Accord de Nouméa*, ya know, the Noumea Agreement on Kanak identity that we signed with the gains we made from the struggle, transfer of powers, local employment, the nickel factory in the North, citizenship, the flag and all that. With the referendum on independence at the end of the process. Well, anyway, what I'm talking about, it's all there, in our paper. Cos see this, sis, even me, Lila, crazy as I am, I still read every single issue of our paper. To keep informed, yeah, but also to stick it to all those assholes who think, just because you're a Kanak woman with a bad reputation, you can't think! The cheek of it, I tell you!

'You see, little sista, it's the first time I've spoken to you just to tell you a bit about the crazy state of mind I'm in right now but, ya know, I've seen you around town plenty of times with all the comrades, selling our paper on the street. Sometimes I feel like joining you but I don't want to dishonour you and the movement and the cause as well. With the

---

11 Bichlamar term for a kava bar. (Transl.)

12 *ibid.*

13 Accord de Nouméa signed in 1998 (Transl.)

way I look, ya know, Lila flashy chick, Lila trashy trick, if you see what I mean. And sometimes, when I'm not too out of it, I'm there, I march with you guys in all our protest demos, I'm there, live performance, sista! *Ah là là!* Specially for the nickel factory up north and specially against racism towards us Kanak women. Remember the photo of Miss Kanaky with the chimp head those miserable little fascist assholes stuck on the net. But anyway, just look at how they represent us, day in day out, in their cartoons and their comic strips! OK, OK fine, if it's for laughs, like they say; but tell me who's laughing at who every time, and just what is it they're insinuating. Because, look, let's get real here, behind all that stuff, what's behind it all is the way we Kanak women, and our Kanak people, we always get looked down on in our own country. Or worse still, not considered at all. Ignored. Look around this place, here this evening, there's only us here! Where're all the others? It's always the same, everything we do, we always end up on our own. And them too. When we have a funeral in one of our villages, where are they? You never see them. We go to their churches though, we go to their cemeteries, their schools! They force us to go. We always have to go to them; never the other way round. Not on your life. And you know, all that, well it comes from the old apartheid system, the famous Indigenous Code our old folks went through. So here, in Kanaky, we better keep on singing, 'no more apartheid', sing it out like our black brothers in other places. Becos all that's still a reality here in Kanaky, behind all the handshakes, all the kissy kissy, lovey doveys and the signed paper agreements. Yeah, sista, actually we still get treated like nothings in our own country, here in Kanaky.

'Cos let me tell you, the one and only thing all these dudes are interested in is our nickel. That's it. Full stop. And obviously, their businesses, their shops and all that stuff, eh. And on that score, you can bet your bottom dollar on it, men are all the same. Mean as, when it comes to their big bucks and big deals. Cos The Rock, like they call our island, is a very juicy morsel, believe you me. Very mouth-wateringly juicy. And we've got no idea just how juicy cos they never let us in on the game. Not in the big league. Yep, it's always big bizness with a heap of profits for their big companies, how do you call 'em again, in your paper? Yeah – multinationals, that's it. And now we're in on the deal, with a good partnership going on up north and down south, now they're gonna tip their shit from the mine into the Havannah Canal. Good Lord, into the canal, my sister, the passage where all our ancestors leave from, ya know! Where's it all leading, I ask you? Well I dreamt about it, dreamt about the place. There was a country floating in oily water with men sitting in it, and their yams growing upright in it! And I could see them from a high, high place, like from the top of a high mountain or standing on a giant's shoulders! And you see, that's the kind of dream that really scares the shit outa me. *Ah là là!* Really gives me the creeps!

'*Aauu!*[14] Ya know, sista, I'm just telling you all this so you'll be encouraged to carry on, ya know, cos you might not guess it but I, Lila, Li-li-Lila Tra la li la, I grew up there in the mine and I've been bumming round town like this, tryin'a keep my head above water since I left home cos of bad family business. I'm not gonna talk about that stuff though, too grubby. Too disgusting. That's what sends me off onto these crazy trips. And, ya know, sometimes I think one day they're gonna get me, gonna take me off somewhere and slit my throat, bump me off, suicide me an' my big mouth. Or maybe I'm gonna end up in the nuthouse. like in that play our bro wrote, ya know. He's one clever dude, don't ya reckon? Specially when he talks about all the shit we have to put up with, us Kanak women, ya know. All we go through. I mean it's true, man! And I don't even have kids and thank God for that, cos man, can you imagine what a mess that'd be! *Ah là là!* And even with all my own crazy stuff to deal with and the rest, I always make sure I never miss his plays. *Aauu*, sista, did you see what happened to Corilen in *Where is Justice?* When you think that kinda thing goes on here in Kanaky, in our own home country! And then there's *The Last Nightfall*, the destruction of the village by the chief for his nest-feathering mining project, all that! *Ah là là!* I still get goosebumps thinking about it.

---

14 *Aauu!* common interjection. (Transl.)

'But anyway, yeah, to get back to me running away all the time, well I took off from home just at the start of the Troubles, you know, when we blocked off the roads an' stuff. There was a roadblock just outside the *tribu* [15]on the road to the mine. And I started running away from home with my boyfriend and my cuzzies so we could cook and take food to the ones that were manning this roadblock, see. But, how can I explain it? Actually, I didn't really know what was going on – I mean, why. Why? Because our olds at home and the whole family, well, they weren't exactly on our side, ya see.

'*Ah là là!* Man, it was bad news sometimes at home, with their off-the-planet paranoia and their crazy red white an' blue bla bla bla. It's a wonder they didn't barricade themselves into their houses. And man did they go on and on. The bullshit about the ones on the roadblock, I tell you! I needed beans to stick in my ears so I could stop hearing it all, cos all I could think about was my mate who was up there with them. But for me and the others who were just finishing the school year, it was just about the end of classes an' all that, start of the summer holidays. Perfect opportunity to start partying it up. Party time! *Aauu!* Make love not war, that ring a bell, sista? So anyway, for us, it meant bye-bye teachers, bye-bye homework, bye-bye rules and detentions an' all that! It was total unruliness and revolt with the whole of Kanaky caught up in the struggle. And for me, most of all, it was bye-bye to my olds and hel-lo freedom!

'An' another thing, I remember the first time I arrived on the roadblock and I saw the flag and I said to my cousin,

— What country's flag is that?

— What, you don't know our flag? *Aauu!* Sorry cuzzy babe but, hey, time you woke up there, get with it sis! That there flag flying in front of you, that's the Kanaky flag. Our flag, the flag of the Kanak people, of the people of this here country! That's the Kanaky flag, Lila! But we already told you cuzzies, it's time you all got yourself a bit better informed, ya know. Cos it's a bit rough when a person doesn't even recognise the flag of their own country. But, anyway,

15 The people and the territory of the village.(Transl.)

there it is, now you know, you can see it there in front of you, Lila, the Kanaky flag.

'But anyway, I sure wasn't going back home after that, cos things had gotten too impossible between my olds and me. They even tried to get the cops to bring me back but, well, you can imagine, they had other fish to fry, with the revolt raging throughout Kanaky, sweeping over the country like a tsunami. With paratroopers, the army, mobile troops, cops, dudes in masks, commando operations, guns and rifles all over the place. Cops raiding people's houses, paratroopers and tanks coming and going, army trucks and jeeps! And that's not counting the green berets and the GIGN[16] sharpshooters. And the Puma choppers over the villages all day, swooping down between the pines and the coconut palms. *Ah là là!* The place was a real war zone. So that, for a while there, all you saw was soldiers and cops and choppers in kids' drawings at the Kanak people's school. But at least the Kanaky flag was there too, to make up for the rest.

'Because later, when the Front decided to set up basic political economic and educational structures for the start of the next school year, wherever it was possible, my boyfriend and I joined some other young ones in his tribe up in the valley and we helped organise the local EPK, the *école populaire kanak*. Ah, sis, I loved that school. Man, I loved that school. The school that was born out of that time. The time of the struggles. This school was nothing like the one I'd just dropped out of. This school really opened my eyes to my own identity. Where I come from, who I am, where I'm going. That was where I learned to stand tall. And to be with others. The school of my dreams! Us girls were with the old women in the storytelling and weaving workshops where they taught us at the same time as they taught the children. And so I learned weaving as well. But first I learned how to take off the spikes from pandanus leaves, how to dry them, roll them or soften them in boiling water. We used to get them from the *tribus* along

16 Special intervention unit of the Gendarmerie Nationale. (Transl.).
    French equivalent of the SAS

the coast, together with coconuts and shellfish that we women would gather while the men talked, as usual – same old, same old! Well, man, did we weave some mats and bags and hats! Same with coconut leaves, we made balls, *pola*[17] and *bénô*[18] baskets and mats, and all that to sell at the EPK market.

'But the thing I remember best that I learned from the old women back in the time of the struggles is the stories. All the stories that are still inside me today and that I'm always telling – here, there and everywhere. That's why they call me 'Lila the storyteller' or 'Lila rubbish teller', or probably worse – but anyway, I couldn't give a damn. Cos it's my way of standing tall. And everything I know, I learned from the old women back in the time of the struggles. You wouldn't believe, sis, all the things we learned from all our old grandmothers up the valley! It was a dreamland for women, like we were in girl heaven.

'Apart from that, us girls used to design and make our clothes or sew mission dresses on the sewing machine we bought for the women's group, with money from our sales. And then there were all the recipes we tried out, selling the cakes at school or at the cooperative, along with bags of *manioc* or grated banana and *bougnas*.

'And all that was on top of school, working the gardens, going on protests, and attending meetings: meetings to set up our political programme, school progress report meetings, and political education meetings with the working groups from other tribes. And to get to them, we would stay off the main road to avoid anti-independence whites, cops and paras, and take shortcuts across walking tracks. Sometimes when we didn't have a torch at night, man, did it put the wind up us when it was pitch black up in the forest and we'd come across what I call an encounter of the third kind, ya know, where you'd hear noises like in a school playground or people bathing, shouting and laughing like kids horsing around at midnight in the forest! Afterwards, when we'd tell the grandmothers about it, they

---

17 Large basket woven from coconut leaves, in the *cî* language (Transl.).
18 Floor covering, in the *cî* language.(Transl.)

used to say not to be afraid cos it was just the forest people happy to see us passing through. Any case, man, did we do some walking! *Ah là là!* The stuff we did in the time of the struggles, sis!

'But to get back to the question of political education. To start with, I didn't exactly find it easy. Didn't quite gel. But it was compulsory for all the organisers of the EPK, so I couldn't get out of it. Actually, it was like another language to me because of all the stuff I was hearing at home every day from the olds, who were against us. But in the end it taught me how to tell the difference between, say, a slave, a serf and the proletariat. Or between people who are dominated, and the exploited and the colonised. Or between different kinds of exploitation, say the day to day exploitation of a working couple and the domination of the woman by the man in a couple. Luckily for me I had my mate to explain everything over to me again at home, cos he was right into it, like a fish in water, because of what his family and his clan had been through. Besides, you probably know, today he's one of our leaders. Like they say, it was bound to happen cos he grew up with politics since he was knee-high, with his fathers and grandfathers. Anyway, you don't need me to tell you, sis, men have always had everything. Starting with the right to speak. Right?

Apart from that, we had plantations for self-sufficiency. Yam gardens, taros and sweet potato. Manioc, bananas and sugar cane. And veggie gardens with lettuces, cabbage, Chinese cabbage, spring onions, leaks and carrots. *Ambreuvade* peas and chokos and pumpkins, sticky cabbage and watercress. *Ah là là*, sis! Did we ever work the land in the time of the struggles!

And that's not counting sun coffee harvest to make money for the school and the party. Man, we had the time of our lives up in the coffee plantation, specially after the election results cos we knew the Front was in tough negotiations with the French government for a new statute for our country and that it all depended on us being active on the ground. So up there, at the coffee plantation, anyone who could manage to get Radio Djiido would be blaring out the latest news and it'd come with 'old farts and assholes and dirty traitors' and all sorts of other insults

61

against those that called us rapists and murderers and terrorists. I mean, honestly, look at us here, in this *nakamal*. Look at me, sis! Do I look like a terrorist to you? Get away! What a load of bullshit!

But the most precious gift of life from those times was my baby. My son. My gift of life, from the earth and the sky. The son I had with my mate, and who also belonged to the old women and girls who spoiled the hell out of me when I was carrying – before, during and after I gave birth. I didn't have to worry about a thing when his father was off at meetings or away on party business: the grandmothers and mothers, the sisters and cousins, daughters and nieces were all there for me. Women are there. They're always there for you. And I didn't want to go to the medical centre because of what might happen on the road with the cops, the paras and the army and all! There was even a case of a mum-to-be who was held up by a road check who died having her baby. And to us, it was just one more way of eliminating us and our children, if you know what I mean. So I was dead set on having my baby at home in the *tribu* and on him being delivered by our women, since they are the ones who've brought us into the world, ever since the world began. *Ah là là!* I've never taken so many herbs in my life, sis, as when I was carrying with my son. Specially sticky plants, Kanak cabbage. And afterwards, it all went so well; the same day, I was back on my feet, holding my baby against me, like this! *Aauu!* I can still smell him, the lovely baby smell of him here, in my breast! cos when it came to feeding him, with all the stuff the old women made me drink, I had heaps and heaps of milk, my breasts were full of it, full to the brim! That's what made my baby so gorgeous and fat. You shoulda seen him, sis! And he was such a playful little boy, such a mischief, always laughing and singing. About everything and nothing. And later, sis, for the five years we had him on earth with us, during all those years of grace that God granted us in the time of the struggles, we made sure we celebrated his birthday every year with the family, up in the tribe. Always with reggae hits by Bob and other black brothers going full blast: *Redemption Song, Buffalo Soldier, Many Rivers to Cross, No Woman No Cry*, that we'd end up all singing along to, with the bros and the sistas from up home.. And my son too, learned to sing a few lines, mostly to get a laugh out of his nannies and pops from up there.

We stayed on a hill and from there you could see the river. After lunch, I would have a siesta with my son under the *tabou* tree in the courtyard with all its flowers that smell so good at the end of the year. And once, I dreamt I was swimming near a little canoe where my baby was sleeping. We were just letting ourselves be carried along by the current of the river. And, suddenly, I was woken by the realisation that my son was no longer in the canoe. I started to look for him and got caught in the net of a fisherman, under the mimosas, down by the sea. And the first time I went down to the bay over there, down by the wreck, I recognised the place of my dream. And, since I'd never been there before, I asked my mother about it when I next saw her, at a funeral. She said that actually I had been there once, when I was very small, with her and her girlfriends and cousins from the mine. And that when we left the place, I had been really sick. I wouldn't stop crying, kept having nightmares and refused to eat. She and my aunty took me to a grandmother who healed me. While I was carrying, with my baby, when Aunty Léna came to see me up in the *tribu*, she told me she was sure I'd have a boy and asked me to name him after the son she had lost, Tom. *Ah là là!* Still gives me the shivers to think about it, sista!

But sometimes, when I dream about my son, it's as if he was still here, here in my arms, like back then, looking up at me with his smiling eyes while I rock him to sleep like this, hold him close against me, with the lullaby that one of the grandmothers from up home used to sing:

Go to sleep
My beautiful baby
Born of the time of the struggles
Don't you cry
The ogre is nigh

63

Listening and waiting
Under the stone of war

Don't shed a tear
The ogre is near
Listening and waiting
By the river
For his hour to come

Go to sleep
My beautiful baby
Born of the time of the struggles

'After my son was buried under the *tabou* tree, that same grandmother planted a little *bancoul* next to him so he could climb up it and play in the branches, because we are all fruits of the *bancoul* tree.

'Afterwards, sista, after I lost him at the age of five, from a bad flu, it was all over for me. Some people reckoned I should go and see someone cos maybe it had come from back home, evil-eye maybe, because of politics, all the stuff we were involved in. I wouldn't go cos we weren't doing anything wrong, we were struggling for our people, for the independence of our country, for our dignity, for justice and freedom. What's wrong with that, sis? And then, it wouldn't have brought my son back, anyhow. And then I wasn't interested, I was in too much pain from the loss of my son that happened so fast and knocked me to the ground. Like a bird that's lost its wings. For good.

Ah là là, sis, when he passed away, in the night, really, really late, it reminded me of the famous passage from Victor Hugo, in *Les Misérables* that our French teacher told us about in college, just before the Troubles started. I learned it by heart and bits of it came back to me, like a lullaby in the night: 'He appeared to be having a great time... The barricade was shaking; he was singing. He was neither a child nor a man: he was a strange fairy child... And still a bullet, better aimed or more treacherous than the others, finally hit the will-o'-the-wisp child… He raised his two arms in the air, looked off in the direction whence the bullet had come, and began to sing: I've fallen to the ground, blame it on… He never finished… This great little spirit had flown away.' It's the death of Gavroche.

And that's when I started to become a serious consumer of alcohol and tobacco. And then weed, when I could get it. It was the only thing that could make me forget my little one who had left me forever. Of course his father did everything he could to pull me out of it, so we could make it together, as he used to say. I can tell you, sis, he did everything, but I mean everything to pull me out of it, and with all the patience he has. Cos he used to say that the struggle also means being responsible for your own problems at home and dealing with them. The struggle against yourself. That's the hardest one of all. And that's where I lost the fight, sis. The father of my son, he made it, he went through it and came out the other side. And today, I admire him because he followed the path laid out in the time of the struggles. But for me, well I guess there was other stuff behind it, all the other shit I went through before. And, like they say, "the one who does you wrong eats out of the same plate".

'Obviously, there came a day when my mate'd had enough of seeing me totally off my face and he took off with another sista, a staunch supporter of the cause, really stable and responsible just like him. And it was much better that way, for him and for his work. Cos where I was at right then, I could've gone off with anyone at all, I really, really didn't give a shit about anything any more. Just wanted my baby back.

'And that's how I ended up in the arms of the old man, who found me one day at nightfall by the river. He pulled me down into the reeds, then into the water. And he did it to me all night. And I loved it, sista! You can't imagine how much I loved it! Hell, I'd never known anything like it, even in our best moments with my mate. And you know what? It reminded me of what they say in the stories about bringing up a child. They say a child grows by being dunked in water then put back on dry land. In any case, the next day after this long night when the old man kept dunking me then putting me back on dry land, I was a changed woman. I don't know if it was because of everything he did to me in the water and on dry land but after that I had to follow him. I had become his creature. His object. His plaything. Or rather the slave of my own senses. The slave of my own pleasure. The flesh is weak, sista.

'And that's how the fisherman caught me in his net like in my dream. Still gives me goosebumps to think of it. *Ah là là!* And that's how I ran away with him to this place and ended up staying for a long while in his wreck, down there at the bay. And sometimes, I still go back down there, to the wreck when I'm really, really in need.

'Right, well sis, enough of me dumping my life story on you for one evening. Hope you enjoy the rest of yours. Good luck, sis, and whatever you do, be strong! The struggle goes on!'

The girl was just leaving when Tom asked one of his mates who Lila was.

— She's the storyteller. 'Lila in Wonderland'. Others call her the barefoot bardessa. Or Lily of the Valley, our Lady of Stories. But actually, her name's Delilah, yeah, as in Samson's wife.

And later, when he was introduced to her as having just returned from Sarajevo with the army, she laughed and said, 'So, handsome soldier boy, you been over there too, in Sarajevo. Reason I mention it is I happen to have an aunt who went there on a church trip. And when she got back, she told me she'd been in Sarajevo but she didn't know she'd been in Yugoslavia. And when I assured her Sarajevo was in Yugoslavia and that if she was talking about her trip around the place she'd better make sure and remember it cos if she keeps on doing like she did with me, saying she knows she's been to Sarajevo but doesn't know she's been to Yugoslavia, well people are gonna think she doesn't know where she's at and maybe she's losing it.

So then, soldier boy, how do the snipers operate over there? You know, these sharpshooters that are supposedly afraid of nothing? I remember that, when our history teacher was teaching us about the rise of nationalism in the Balkans before the Second World

66

War, she used to say that the Serbs were real staunch nationalists, proud people, ya know, with total integrity and totally focused on their cause! And that even the Germans never managed to take over the country, cos Tito and his rebel communists had chucked out all their hatchet-men and their Nazis. And that afterwards, Tito himself gathered together the provinces into a federation to create Yugoslavia. He even went on to become a great leader of what they used to call Third World Countries, back then when they held their first big conference on decolonisation up in Indonesia, in Bandung, in the fifties, with himself, Tito, and Chou En-Lai, Nasser and Nehru. You know, the great leaders of those countries they also used to call non-aligned states in respect of the Cold War between the USA and the USSR. But anyway, all that stuff, I learned it from *ba* Kassim – *ba* means father, the word is actually *babak* – so *ba* Kassim, the grandfather of my best friend Mina, who's Javanese, who told us all about that stuff when we were kids. He also told us how, over there, in their country, they fought with their bamboo canons against the Dutch to win their independence. And under the guidance of their president, Ahmed Soekarno. Soekarnoputri, who's often on the radio, that's Soekarno's daughter. And *ba* Kassim, *ba* Sarimin and all the old *ba* who worked for the settlers, they all had a photo of president Soekarno in their house. Even after General Suharto took power and the repression started. I know, because I used to hang out with Mina and her family all the time. That's how I learned a few words of their language: *Saya Lila*, I am Lila. *Salam. Ya. Tidak. Permisi. Sampai jumpa.* Goodmorning. Yes. No. Excuse me. Goodbye. She taught me how to count too: *Nol, satu, dua, tiga, empat, lima.* Zero, one, two, three, four, five. And I remember when Mina and I started going out to parties and all that, *ba* Kassim would tell us to be careful, then he would add a phrase with *tiga*, the number three, in it. When I asked Mina what he was saying to us, she answered that it was a phrase from their book, the Koran, from Sourate 111. It means 'the life of this world brings only ephemeral and deceptive joy'. Oh, la, la! I can't begin to tell you, my brother, everything I learnt with Mina

67

from *ba* Kassim! Like the old people back home in the *tribu*, he was a wellspring of knowledge and wisdom.

And, as if she suddenly remembered something, Lila clapped her hands and said 'If you please, ladies and gentlemen, would you kindly give me just a moment's attention; this evening, I'm gonna change registers a bit and I'm gonna give you my latest rave as a rap song. It's called 'The prayer of the earth'.

This is the prayer
of our mother earth
land of our ancestors
this is the stone
of the land
of nickel
the call
of big money
of fast bucks
and mining trucks
eating up our land
for smart cash
tax breaks
ten per cent
for the land
earth
and yam
floating down
the canal
out to sea
polluting
the sea
and the earth
with nickel
and iron
and the nerve

of war
financial empires
rape and plunder
of the worker
canon fodder
for the war
to end wars
of our foot-soldier
ancestors
our volunteer
grandfathers
our worker fathers
out for the count
from the earth
to the sea
of sharks
on the waterfronts
in the ports
of foreign-owned
factories
this is the prayer of
our mother earth
land of our ancestors

The applause in the darkness of the *nakamal* where Lila had performed her 'rave' was so enthusiastic that a little later on she agreed to recite her rap-poem again twice over, encouraged by her drinking mates and other friends and admirers. Later still, Tom caught sight of her in a nightclub 'totally wasted' as she liked to put it. And to his considerable surprise, she snubbed him royally, just as she did the others to whom she had dedicated her rap-poem back in the *nakamal*. One of his girlfriends asked,

— Is that the Lila who sang rap for us in the *nakamal* a little while back? She must be pretty far gone not to even recognise us.

— Don't you believe it! *Lila es la luna.* She's a loony, off the planet, added another of Lila's girlfriends.

— No way, I don't buy it! She's just who she is, in her own world. After all, she can do as she pleases, can't she?

— And she sure does, she sure does, says a third.

— Right on! Lila does what she wants. She's free as the wind, someone else concludes.

Tom and Léna, Mina and all those who knew Lila well give money for the flowers, the customary gift, the coffin and the burial plot in the cemetery, to give the storyteller a good send-off. A pastor who had worked in the *tribu* up the valley during the time of the struggles took the ceremony in memory of what he called 'her years of grace up home', where he used to entrust her with the *tékès*, biblical texts in indigenous languages read by the children at Christmas. Between the prayer, the hymns and before the final commendation, he gave a reading of Chapter VI of the Epistle to the Romans, verses 19–23:

I speak after the manner of men, because of the weakness of your flesh. As ye have presented your members servants to uncleanness and iniquity unto iniquity, so now present your members servants of righteousness unto holiness.

For when ye were the servants of sin, ye were free from righteousness.

What fruit had ye then from those things whereof ye are now ashamed? For the end of those things is death.

But now being made free from sin, and become servants to God, ye have your fruit unto holiness, and the end everlasting life.

For death is the wages of sin; but eternal life is the gift of God through Jesus Christ our Lord.[19]

After the silent procession to the cemetery and before the burial, following Tom's suggestion during the wake at the mortuary, Lila's male and female friends come in turn to say farewell with a few words

---

19 St Paul's Epistle to the Romans, Translation by John Wesley (Transl.)

like the *tékès*[20] that Tom himself had recited in his younger years, back in his *tribu* up in the hills. And it is Tom who begins:

Matthew, 13:23: The one who received the seed that fell on good soil is the man who hears the word and understands it. He produces a crop, yielding a hundred, sixty or thirty times what was sown.

Another friend continues:

Psalm 144:4: *Man is like a breath; his days are like a fleeting shadow.* Mina and a Maghrebi friend of Tom's, from his time in Sarajevo, take it in turn to read verses from the Koran, the Sourates XC, XCI, XCIII, XCIV:

SOURATE XC

The City
In the name of God:
he who grants mercy,
the Merciful
12. And what will explain to thee,
the path that is steep?
13. It is:
– freeing the bondman;
14. Or the giving of food in a day of privation
15. To the orphan with claims of relationship,
16. Or to the indigent down in the dust.

---

20 Text in several Kanak languages particularly used to refer to a biblical text. (Transl.)

SOURATE XCI

The Sun
In the name of God:
he who grants mercy,
the Merciful
1. By the Sun and his glorious splendour;
2. By the Moon as it follow him;
3. By the Day as it shows up the Sun's glory;
4. By the Night as it conceals it;
5. By the Firmament!
 – And the wonderful structure he has bestowed on it–
6. By the Earth
– And the wide expanse with which he has endowed it–
7. By the Soul,
- And the proportion and order he has given it
Inspiring in it the libertine and the pious! (...)

SOURATE XCIII

The Glorious Morning Light
In the name of God:
he who grants mercy,
the Merciful

1. By the Glorious Morning Light! ...
2. And by the Night when it spreads its mantle!
3. Your Lord Hath not forsaken thee, nor is He displeased!
4. And verily the Hereafter will be better for thee than the present.
5. And soon will Your Lord give thee that wherewith
thou shalt be well-pleased.
6. Did He not find thee an orphan
– and give thee shelter and care?

7. And He found thee wandering
– and He gave thee guidance.
8. And He found thee in need
the image we have
– and made thee rich.
9. Therefore treat not the orphan
– with harshness.
10. Nor repulse the petitioner
– unheard.
11. But the Bounty of thy Lord
– rehearse and proclaim!

SOURATE XCIV

The Opening
In the name of God:
he who grants mercy,
the Merciful

1. Have We not expanded thee thy breast?
2. And removed from thee thy burden
3. The which did gall thy back?
4. And raised high the esteem in which thou art held?
5. So, verily, joy is close to sorrow.
6. Yes, joy is close to sorrow.
7. Therefore, when thou art free from thine immediate task
– get up, go and pray
8. And seek thy Lord with all your heart.

Then, taking turns, the other friends read the verses of their farewell poem to Lila:

Epitaph for Lila

Here lies
Lila,
fallen speaker
of our
 oral tradition
infamous
 oral voice
famished female
endless
(m)orality
speaking
the destiny of
mothers
of this earth

Lila
flower of speech
strangled
down
by the sea

Lila
heavy
with the perfume
of dark
memory

Lila
victim
of man
at the criminal
hour

Lila
tell me
your true tale
of woman
on earth

Lila
fill me
with your
crazy
story

Lila
Carry me away
with you
to the sound
of your voice

And from one story
to the next
May justice
be done
In the end

for the wandering
story teller
of the streets with her
elephant memory

my fate
interests
none
but the social work
professional

no, no Doc
my illness
isn't fatal
poverty
is not fatality

so tell me then
why is it
in this town
the excluded
are all black

or brown
excluded
from the Island
and the Sea
to die

victims
of the jungle
whose king
is called
man

my hope
is dying
in the
face of
the well-fed

dance
of death
dance of

Love
for a passer-by
passing by
walk on by
citizen
don't you
look me
in the eye

no night
or day
in this
head
adrift
in time

one day
love
will
triumph
over my
nothingness

over the void
the gaping hole
of the
global
system

and they tell me
I'm to blame
if I got nothing
I better just
go home

but home
is here
with my son
on the bancoul tree
in the forest

My home is
here in Kanaky
my country
land of
my ancestors

After the burial, Tom and Léna are surprised not to have seen the old fisherman. They remember how he would often say to them 'sometimes you see me, sometimes you don't'. But they didn't see him again, neither before their departure for the *tribu*, nor after.

Chapter 4 – The Hut

Safely tucked away inside their bubble, Tom and Léna are inseparable. But Léna is conscious of the watching eyes and the rumours broadcast over the bush radio of the extended family. When she happens to meet her ex-boyfriend (the young soldier) one afternoon after she finishes work she decides it's better to explain things, out of respect for him and to ease her conscience. Actually, their meeting is no coincidence.

His questioning of his female cousins, who in fact knew no more than he did, had resulted in only the vaguest of answers. In frustration, and since he didn't know of any other way of contacting her, he had come to wait for her in the street, opposite the villa where she cleaned for an elderly lady. This unexpected meeting made things easier for her, saving her from having to go through the break-up ritual while still not knowing quite how to tell him. It meant she could remain herself, just as calm and serene as their relationship had been. The words she uttered, as she looked him straight in the eye, came spontaneously. He thanked her for being so frank. Then he wished her every happiness with his cousin and walked off back to his barracks.

Totally absorbed by their passion, Tom and Léna hardly go out – apart from a few brief unplanned visits to some of their closest friends. They stay away from town, avoiding unwelcome encounters and the spiteful tongues of the local gossipmongers, who sit perched on the benches of the town square, waiting to inject passersby with their witches' venom. The lovers stay cramped up inside Tom's tiny room in a rundown apartment building and, on the weekend, squat in the hillside garden hut belonging to one of Léna's aunties. Tom is overcome by his feelings, carried away by his senses. Nothing can mar his head-over-heels happiness. He is totally immersed in the rhythms of their lovers' games. They are like some miraculous, stimulating drug that leaves him in a drunken ecstasy, in a state where his entire existence is in the here and now, a spatio-temporal present that owes nothing to a specific place or time. The confines of the room reduce their lovers' universe and force them to bond closer together. Being shut up with her in this cramped space turns him on more than anything else. Having her totally to himself, he can set about demolishing her last remaining defences and inhibitions, one by one. For it's now clear to him that, in spite of her ardent passion, Léna has yet to learn the ways of pleasure. So he sets about initiating her into the discovery of her own body, of herself as a sexual being. He leaves her moaning and crying out in response to his urgently questioning lips as he explores every inch of her being. Submerged, crushed, she is like a child's toy that he shakes and rattles and turns over and over, until she is spent. She is satiated, overflowing with orgasmic pleasure, and then, before she knows it, he's doing it to her again and again.

Though when he tries teasing her with questions about the things she used to do with his soldier cousin, the sudden look of sadness in her eyes forces him to stop short and apologise. Up until now, his sex life has consisted of brief, furtive encounters behind the back of a negligent lover or an absent husband, or else hot, steamy affairs where he sometimes found himself overwhelmed by his own fantasies. With Léna, he wants to take things slowly, break down her resistance one step at a time. Not wanting to embarrass her or force things and scare her off, he stops asking questions and avoids trying to get to the bottom of this strange way she has of stopping short, holding back, in a mute refusal tinged with clashing desire and pleasure. He wants nothing from her that she doesn't freely consent to give. He's relying on being able to give her enough of himself to erase her apprehension and ease her fear of living. He's counting on his optimism and enthusiasm to reassure her and help her regain her faith in herself.

Sure that time is on his side, that they have their whole lives ahead of them, Tom brushes aside all thoughts of the past. He finds it hard to understand how anyone can persist in trying to hold on to what is irredeemably lost. Unburdened by the weight of the past, his unique vantage point is firmly in the present. Thus, his former flings and passions have flown from his unfaithful memory, leaving him in a state of inner peace that gives him entirely to Léna. The mutinous, mocking voices of those bygone 'mornings-after' have fallen silent, paving the way for an almost spiritual transformation so that now, each morning, he awakes a new man, seeing the world in a new light. The irresistible desire to get up and leave after a night of love-making that used to dog him has miraculously disappeared. Right now he's living in the present in a state of unfathomable plenitude that has taken possession of his entire being and which he wouldn't give up for anything in the world. Until now he has limited his contact with women to a few words and gestures, the bare necessities required by the pursuit of pleasure, without really bothering to stop and consider what they might have felt. With Léna it's a different story, for although he is sure that this state of inner peace has created a closeness that bonds them far beyond the pleasure of sex, it still doesn't stop him wanting to gain access to that other place that sometimes tears her brutally away from him, even if only for a barely perceptible blink of an eyelid. He's got to find the key to this place. Swears he will find it and deliver her from it, once and for all.

Tom has a confused sense that there is some kind of link between Léna's fleeting absences, her recurring nightmares, and the occasional sudden withdrawals he can't help noticing during their most intense love-making. But he is so firmly anchored in the here and now that he has some trouble connecting the phenomenon to Léna's past, even just as far back as the break-up with his cousin or the death of her mother. He knows how caring his cousin is, and he is convinced he has cured Léna of her grief. Moreover, he has personally spoken quite frankly to him of their relationship, as protocol demands, and it is true that being the elder gives him the upper hand. He is unconcerned about his own past, which he sees as dead and gone, so is not in the least jealous of Léna's past, which he considers none of his business. The present is a clean slate. Yesterday was yesterday, today is today, tomorrow will be tomorrow. As far as he's concerned, the equation is clear. But the multi-dimensional problem hounding Léna is right there, in the middle of their today, plum in the middle of their living present. Still, he has trouble putting a finger on the heart of the problem, especially since she herself appears unable or unwilling to share it with him. It is true, he's doing all he can, taking the time to think it through, trying to get to the bottom of it; but it's the first time he's had to solve this kind of problem with a woman. All the old excuses he would employ to avoid uncomfortable female troubles are gone now, lost indeed in the disappearing wake of dead years. And yet, strangely, he can't manage to project the image of the two of them together as a couple, into a future where this problem would no longer exist. It's particularly within the confines of his room that he senses Léna's reluctance. He sees immediately that its source lies far beyond the lack of privacy of their circumstances, the constant comings and goings on the stairwell, along the corridors and on the landings of the overcrowded building. They are both sufficiently familiar with the rules of the game in their world to go off and do their love-making somewhere else if need be. And he is more or less sure he's not stifling her with his own ardour, which he's reasonably good at controlling. Nor can he believe her reluctance is due to a lack of experience. He thinks he's known enough women to be able to distinguish between territory that is off limits and what are simply areas of lack of confidence and inexperience. He understands how far he can go with them, how to recognise the uncharted territory in each one. His own fascination with the forbidden is doubled by the challenge that Léna's involuntary resistance poses to his male pride, drawing him like a magnet even more strongly to her.

On the other hand, her nightmares leave him in a state of bewildered refusal. For, even though he can admit that dreams may offer a means of reliving the past, perceiving the present and foreseeing the future, he is somewhat uncomfortable with the dream world. As his own memory tends to dispense with the past, and he is far too firmly anchored in the present, too strongly wedded to reality, he has very few memories of either his dreams or nightmares. Generally, no more than the odd flash ever leaves a lasting impression. Like when he sees and feels himself, soaring like some great bird above forest or city. Other feelings that sometimes creep into his nocturnal visions are the terrifying sensation of being bogged down, like trying to run in slow motion through quicksand pursued by unknown assailants; or the feeling of vertigo that sometimes grips him, where he is falling into a void. The worst ones are where he tries to move, or wants to cry out, but is frozen to the spot, speechless. But he always manages to bring himself out of his nightmare moments by moving his toes, like the old nannies told him to do. They told him, too, that the falling sensation of dreams originates from the crumbs from his last meal, dropped from a height by an ant as it scurries away with them, maybe from the top of a blade of grass, a branch or a wall. They reckoned that the pursuers in a person's dreams are sorcerers, seeking to cast evil spells. The same is true of fishermen. But Tom has long since ditched all that rubbish, as he calls it, and the only such belief to which he gives the slightest credence comes from one old relation who was wont to declare that never, never would she fall sick or die to please some sorcerer – male or female – who didn't bring her into this world.

And yet, one particular dream image, somewhat indistinct, like the rest of his memory of his past life, has long haunted him. He was driving back alone from a late-night party when he began to fall fast asleep at the wheel; he stopped the car on the side of the road, at the top of a pass. There he had a dream about an old man, some grandfather whose face he couldn't recognise. The old man opened the rear passenger door and unceremoniously got in and sat down, right in the middle of the back seat. He seemed to be waiting for Tom to turn around, so that he could deliver the message that he had obviously come to give him. At that point, Tom heard him whisper quite clearly in his right ear, in his native tongue, '*This is where they'll be waiting for you*'. Whereupon, the stranger's face filled the rear-vision mirror with a sardonic grin. Tom woke with a start, turned the key in the ignition and drove off in a cloud of dust. Later, when he recounted the dream to his young cousin, the latter advised him to take special care when driving over the hill passes – the old man was warning him that he could have a serious accident there. Tom promised to bear it in mind just so as not to upset his cousin. But ever since he had met the old fisherman, in whose face he recognised the grandfather of his dream, he had indeed been thinking about it.

Even if Léna responds as best she can to Tom's passionate attentions within the confines of his tiny room, she still can't shake the impression that the place puts her at the mercy of some of her worst nightmares. When she tries to work out the link between these nocturnal fears and the uncontrollable reluctance that tears her from him at the height of their love-making, it's as if she is standing in front of a wall that shuts her off from a part of herself. She is sure there is something, somewhere, that she can't yet put a finger on, can't yet remember, that her memory must have mislaid, somewhere way back before her mourning for her mother and her vague sense of guilt at having gone from one cousin to the other. It must lie far beyond the brutal intrusion of pleasure, which has revealed to her another self that she is having trouble recognising. She has nothing against this new twin sister, eager to follow her lover's lessons in the discovery of her body. For she has found that love-making has brought her peace of mind in the hillside garden hut, or outside on the dry grass, under the stars or by moonlight.

On weekends and holidays, Tom and Léna take over the place and more or less take charge of their Auntie's gardening chores. So much so, that she happily leaves them to it and goes off somewhere else to clear another patch of land with her old girlfriends.

Léna is by far the most active, both when it comes to digging, cutting and weeding and when the yam, taro, cassava and *ambrevade* peas are planted. With the machete deftly sharpened by Tom, she slashes away at tall grass and bushes and works the soil that her companion has dug, breaking up the heavy clods, raking and hoeing until the earth is like fine dark seeds that she lets run gently through her fingers. She plants vegetable seedlings and cuttings with all the patience in the world. And, whenever she gets a chance, she fills a can and waters them a little, with Tom following after her with a bigger can. And so, in this way, the hut and the fields become their refuge, their secret hillside garden.

When she's not busy fetching and carrying, Léna will be squatting down somewhere, bent over or sitting on the ground, working the soil, her gestures and movements attuned to its various shapes and forms as it runs through her fingers. She is like a magician fascinated by her own creations, filled with wonder at the living green of her fields against the arid dryness of the surrounding hills. Tom is likewise overwhelmed by the beauty of their own private paradise, their 'hanging gardens of Babylon' as he calls them, in an ironic allusion to the capitalist system lampooned in countless reggae songs. And often he pushes in between Léna and the earth, taking her by the hand and leading her towards the hut. Or taking her there and then, when his desire for her is too strong – as had happened one day, towards noon down in the shade of the mimosas. There she had let herself go completely, scratching his back and crying out his name.

These mimosas had vaguely reminded her of a place by the sea, a patch of red earth that she glimpsed occasionally in her dreams. Once, she had seen herself in front of a cemetery, at night, carrying a cooking pot. Next thing, it was broad daylight and there she was, in a place by the sea, asking a man for directions. He was none other than the old fisherman. She leaves him and comes to a creek where some small rowing-boats are moored. Leaping from one to the other, in a few short bounds, she is across. Further downstream, one of her cousins is standing in the water. She calls to Léna to give her the fish she's holding in her hand.

But this particular time, when she and Tom are making love, she sees a scene from a story her mother once told her; one that was told to her by an oil-tanker driver. One very hot afternoon, he had picked up a hitchhiker, a woman, who asked him to let her make a comfort stop by a thicket of mimosas. A moment later, he heard a whistle and caught a glimpse of her, standing naked, between their skinny trunks. Without further ado, he leapt out of his tanker, had his way with the woman, then dumped her. The strangest part of it was that, some time after, the driver was killed in an accident, at that very spot. And it was never clear whether it was really a woman, or a fantasy, or the guardian of the place in the Kanak sense of the word. Ashamed of this mental image linked to the memory of her mother, which was bringing her to orgasm, she promised herself never to let herself get caught up again in such fantasies. And Tom, comparing the molten lava of her belly to an erupting volcano, doesn't understand what is going on but makes up his mind to wait as long as is necessary

From these sexual experiences, Léna gradually established a link between the beach bordered by mimosas and a piece of red earth, and the irrepressible malaise she experienced in her love-making with her companion. But she doesn't understand at all what the old fisherman is doing in her dreams. Even though, during their conversation near the wreck, a particular tone in his voice had struck her, like the link in a chain of forgotten memories. Unless he, too, was one of those 'satellites', sometimes nicknamed

'Batman' in the coded language used for speaking about sorcerers. And, like her girlfriends, she thinks about the clairvoyants in the small ads that they consult to find out more about themselves and their future. She also thinks about the women who hold special powers of prevention and cure in the clan, who could help her work out what is going on. For never before, since the death of her mother, has she felt so lost, even abandoned, facing these questions without answers. She continues to keep up a brave face with Tom, who, far from being deceived, sees that she is struggling with insoluble problems – for the moment, at least. He ends up reducing their sexual encounters, so as not to overburden her and to give her the space she needs. He sees himself as having his whole life to draw her gently away from her inner darkness. And he knows he can only do this with her assistance.

By going back over and over past memories, she finally remembers what her mother, Maria, had said to her one day about the aunt whose first name, Helena, and its diminutive, Léna, had become hers. Like her grandmother, who raised her and from whom she has inherited the gift, Helena can translate dreams. 'Your mother is no longer alive, but don't forget that I, Mama Léna, your other mother whose name you carry, am still here, and whatever happens, you can count on me.' These words of consolation were spoken to Léna at her mother's funeral. For both women spent a part of their youth with women who worked in town, from their respective tribes and from elsewhere. A deep understanding developed between them that proved as useful for their relationships with men as for the wild partying of their early years in town. Her mother had met Helena after her return to town from the *tribu*, where another woman had taken her place alongside her companion and their son.

That was the period of half-day work as a house-cleaner, and evenings babysitting for two or three bosses. They would end up leaving before they were thrown out on the spot, for breaking dishes when they were drunk or insulting Madam who was getting laid by her gigolo whenever Monsieur had his back turned. But the wildest evenings sometimes took place in their bosses' villa, when the latter were away on vacation abroad, or 'home' twenty thousand kilometres away. The band of young people would empty the bar and the cellar of everything, before sleeping it off in the living room, or sleeping the sleep of the just in the bedrooms. Occasionally, they would fall asleep completely drunk at a table or in the corner of some nightclub, until they were pushed out at closing time. Afterwards, there were discussions on the pavement till dawn about who would take who home and was going home with whom. Or who was going to the café or the market with whom. On yet other occasions, two of the girls, fighting about a guy they were both getting their knickers in a twist over, had to be separated. Until the cops turned up and the whole lot of them were carted off to spend the night in the lock-up.

And then, one fine morning, they followed a somewhat older woman that many people called affectionately 'granny', and others ´*\ Éva – as did Léna, who knew her well. A caretaker for the property of her boss, on the outskirts of the town, she lived there alone in a two-roomed wooden hut, at the bottom of the garden. She left them the second bedroom, which contained a pandanus mat and two single sprung beds watched over by a pin-up of Marilyn Monroe, who stood out from the other Hollywood glamour-girls stuck on the wall. They brought a breath of youth to the shack, to the great delight of Éva, who liked to laugh and have fun. They vied with one another, making little dishes from the recipes in magazines borrowed from Madam and showing off their culinary talents. Over coffee and at mealtimes, they listened to aunty tell funny stories, and the strange stories of her life in town or of her life before that, up there in the *tribu*. She also knew a good number of traditional tales, stories and lullabies. She made them laugh – telling them snippets about the lives of her friends, like the one who had a fight with her lover and threw his clothes out on the footpath after she had locked him in, shouting out from the street, 'Okay, out you come and show yourself to everyone, now that you're naked as a worm, you dirty pimp!' On the weekends they had games of *belote* or dominos after the meal, or a Sunday siesta to get over the nightclub crawls of Saturday night. Like the Saturday night when her mother met her father. A few months later, he found work in a mining centre, to where she followed him. When little Léna was born, she had two mothers, for, following Éva's advice, Helena had gone with Maria to be at her side during the birth.

Chapter 5 – The Graveyard of Canoes

Mama Léna comes from a long line of builders of outrigger canoes, and she carries their name in her Kanak language. It is also the name of a place beside the sea, where a waterfall cascades down. It is our connection to the land that gives us our identity. The elders of the clan have been leaving their old canoes to die there for generations, ever since the time when the wreck of the craft sailed by the first ancestor became a flat black rock, in the shape of a great canoe. Columnar pines and coconut palms guard the entrance against intrusive visitors lured by the waterfall and the beach below or by the lagoon, so admired for the transparent blue and emerald green of its waters. The aura surrounding the graveyard of the canoes is in no way diminished by the dramatic events of the founding stories linked to the place and passed down from generation to generation. The story goes that the canoe of the first ancestor, buffeted by the winds and the ocean tides, capsized one night and was wrecked; the ancestor and his grand-daughter were the sole survivors. At daybreak, the grand-daughter went looking for her parents and suddenly stopped, stock-still on the sand, before the battered remains of her mother's body, thrown up by the waves. She claims she distinctly heard her mother's voice, warning her that there would be others who would come up out of the sea one day to subject her to the same fate. After that, she became mute and did not speak again until the unexpected arrival of a young stranger, cast up after a cyclone onto the beach, like a gift from the sea. She fell passionately in love with this one and only companion of her own age. They had several sons, whom the grandfather initiated into canoe-building and the secrets of the sea. Their father slipped from the rocks one day and drowned, as the old man had foreseen and told his grand-daughter in repeated predictions. When her grandfather himself disappeared later, in the same way, she stopped talking altogether. She spent her last days sitting on the rocks, staring intently at the waves as if they were coming to carry her off in their turn. Which they did. The versions differ as to the exact circumstances of this disappearance, but all those who tell it conclude that the price of the land is giving what belongs to it back to the sea.

Mama Léna had this story from her paternal grandmother, a great storyteller who recounted all these tales to her and to the other children of the clan as if she had lived them. One evening, the children were all huddled in fear around the fire listening to her tales. They were facing the banyan tree where old mother Tibo lived, an ogress with long pendulous breasts, who could leap out and catch you, just like the ogre of the graveyard of canoes. One of Léna's young cousins, half-asleep by then, asked her,

— So where are we, here?

— What do you mean, 'where are we here?'

— Is this Old Mother Tibo's place or where the ogre lives?

— It's not her place or his place. We're at our place, of course.

— No, no. You're lying! We are at Mother Tibo's 'cos I can see her over there! It's her talking! Over there, look, over there, that's her, she murmured, trembling and pointing to their grandmother, the storyteller, who had overheard her and replied in a hollow voice,

— Oh no! I'm not Mother Tibo. I am the ogre from the graveyard of canoes and I'm looking for a little girl to take away with me aboard my wreck, far, far away, over the stormy seas.

For a long time after the end of the last story, deeply impressed by this scene, Léna was still having trouble falling asleep, although the other children had been snoring away for a long time. Only a slender, bright red flame continued to burn, trembling in the blackness. Then she became aware of the smell of something rotten and she saw the flame grow suddenly narrow-waisted and tall and take on a human form. A scarlet dwarf, a diminutive man-sized, pomegranate-coloured gnome, was silhouetted against the wall of the thatch house. A blood-coloured light radiated from him, revealing grandmother's face. Her posture was one of strange and absolute submission. Never before had she seen her grandmother so.

'Do it! Such is my will!', ordered the dwarf with authority. In the almost inaudible whisper of a slave to her master, the old woman repeated, 'Yes, yes, yes', as she followed, moaning, in the wake of the little flame that was moving toward the door. Then the coconut leaf curtain fell on the heavy gait of a man walking away into the night, to the sound of waves breaking. A little before dawn, a terrible cry woke the children, who saw the grandmother bending over the little girl who had mistaken her for old Mother Tibo the evening before. She asked her what was wrong and drew the child close against her to comfort her, telling her that her mother would be coming to fetch her very soon. But the child cried even harder, screaming that she wanted to leave. Léna realised that she was rejecting any contact with the old woman. She immediately made the connection with what she had seen in the night and, for the first time, she felt afraid of her grandmother.

And so, when her grandmother ordered her to follow the father of the sick girl and go and fetch her mother from the other side of the *tribu*, she obeyed without protest. Even though she had always been afraid of that uncle, who came from another part of the country and spoke to them in French; an uncle whose gaze, reddened by constant diving at sea, sometimes seemed to drill right through her. She didn't know what other people thought about him for she had been much too afraid to talk about him. On the path in front of the canoe cemetery, he told her that he would come back that way with her and the children that afternoon to cast his nets. She waited for him in the shade of a mango tree in the courtyard while he went inside the house and told his partner about the little girl's illness. She heard them arguing and her aunt reproaching him violently saying, 'it was because of what he was doing'. She was screaming that if anything happened to her daughter, she would denounce him. He laughed in her face and retorted that he would make her lots of other children since she liked making them with him so much and that, in fact, he was going to begin right there and then. He closed the door and soon the little girl could hear only moaning and sighing coming from behind the cob walls. Then, very soon, she heard the mocking voice of the man who was taunting her aunt again, 'There, you see, I might just've left another bun in your oven right now. You like it so much, not even the illness or the death of your child will stop me mounting you, because that's all you think about! You come like a bitch when I rape you, you dirty slut! And it's the same with your old witch of a mother. Even at her age she still comes back begging for more in her dried up old hole. Ah, like mother, like daughter! Go on, get a move on now, or that old ogress'll gobble up your daughter. Go on, hurry up and get going!' Not wanting to hear anything more said about her grandmother, Léna left and walked back down the path home ahead of them.

In the afternoon, while she was playing with the other children on the beach, he called her over and told her to go and wait for him over by the pine trees in the canoe cemetery. When he joined her, he forced her to submit completely to his lust on the flat surface of the black rock, then ordered her never to speak of it to anyone or else he would do even worse things to her.

The little cousin died the following day, to the great despair of her aunt, who stood in tears beside the grandmother to receive all the relatives who had come to support her in her grief. In the church, during the sermon, just when the pastor was asking 'O death, where is thy sting? O death, where is thy victory?' Léna surprised the same piercing gaze and curious smile on her uncle's face. After the funeral, the two women were so dazed with grief, the other mothers and aunts had to help them get themselves on their feet and back home. Late in the night, when she was sleeping on the mat on the beaten earth with her uncle, her aunt and her grandmother, she thought she felt fingers and tongues running over her whole body to the same moaning and sighing she had heard during the couple's quarrel.

She escaped the trio when school went back. As a boarder with other female cousins, she returned to the *tribu* only for the holidays. The young girls were united by their efforts to find ways of getting around the restrictions imposed by the extended family and the world of adults, though they dared not challenge these head-on. After the death of her grandmother, her aunt joined a sect to escape the power of 'the outsider uncle', who was still hanging around the *tribu* in pursuit of another of their aunts.

Then, one afternoon, when she was an adolescent, she came upon him unexpectedly as she was passing by a coffee plantation. He pulled her into the bushes. She followed him as if she had been waiting for this for a long time – since the canoe cemetery. She obeyed him in everything – and the more she submitted her body and the more she discovered pleasure, the greater her desire for him grew.

Become his creature, she ran away with him when the other aunt came upon them on the earth floor of the house, where they were deliberately drawing out their pleasure in order to tease her. He dragged her around from one relatives' house to another. His family, embarrassed by being put in this situation, judged him both childish to have become besotted with a young girl, and brazen to dare impose upon them such an inappropriate passion, in defiance of both Christian and customary morality.

He found a job as a gardener for a middle-aged couple. Then, one day, he took her on the rug in the middle of the living room and as they writhed around, entangled together, his bosses arrived home unexpectedly early. Rather than being offended, they pulled the curtains and the adolescent girl became the object of the whole trio's fantasies – and later, of the fantasies of some carefully chosen friends of the couple, including a young entrepreneur who sometimes took photos of their amorous encounters. He made a few copies for the gardener and suggested the possibility of using them against the others. The gardener thought this was just another bit of white man rubbish that had nothing to do with him, but he played along. The two men made sure they themselves were never in range of their little candid camera.

And so they spent many a hilarious moment together, viewing and commenting on the images, laughing themselves to tears. The entrepreneur had business dealings with one of the participants and owed him a considerable sum of money. He claimed that the other man had cheated him, and asked the gardener to be his right-hand man and help get his money back through what was to be their first actual blackmail effort. The gardener was to put the photos in the target's letterbox. When the cops caught him in the act, his companion in crime didn't lift a little finger to help him, and he found himself in prison while the others continued to use and abuse Léna.

Nevertheless, she didn't miss a single visit to the visiting-room where his words, his gaze and his hands upon her through the bars bound them even more tightly together. Every meeting followed a ritual that began with the guard's announcement of the arrival of the 'niece' as the prisoner had called her. Dressed as he had commanded – in this case, in nothing but a mission dress of heavy black fabric buttoned at the front, she would sit in the half-light, on the concrete block that served as a chair, with her eyes lowered. Their fingers would touch and caress each other between the holes in the wire partition, taking in each other's scent in preparation for what was to come. Then he would order her to look at him and asked what treats she had brought for 'uncle' today. Then he'd question her about everything she'd done with the couple before telling her, one by one, all the things he planned to do to her, from the tip of her toes to the

95

top of her head, without leaving out a single part of her body, which he continued to bend to his desire. He wore a pair of nylon shorts, wide enough in the leg to show her everything. He asked her to do the same, to unbutton her dress and open wide what he wanted to see. The fingers of their left hands clasped tight while he filled the young girl's ears with a flood of dirty whisperings. Meanwhile they masturbated with the other hand till they came, the wild spasms of their pleasure exploding behind the walls of the prison. She would totter out, delirious, as he reminded her to do a good job of selling herself again during the week so she could bring sugar and tobacco for uncle at her next visit.

When he got out, they occupied an old fisherman's hut at the water's edge, opposite the wreck of a large boat. Certain nights, at full moon, he would paint their bodies with the juice from macerating leaves and invoke the god of canoes, before taking her in the wreck, which rocked and swayed on the wild waves of their love-making. Afterwards, she would drink the juice so as not to fall pregnant. And so they lived on fresh air and love alone. That is to say, mainly on rice and fish. And they didn't lack for any of the basics, for the fisherman also sold some of his catch. If necessary, she sold herself too, to supplement their daily bread. Seeing her in the arms of others excited him, even more so when this was part of a commercial transaction, and he ended up organising a few drinking parties for just such a purpose. He would joke to their companions about how much she liked it. How she liked it hard, 'specially when it came with hard cash'. Then, one evening, there came along a young man who bore no resemblance to the usual crowd that frequented the wreck. It was quite evident that his only purpose in being there was to accompany the uncle with whom he had arrived. He was good-looking, well-dressed, didn't smoke, didn't drink. He was well-mannered, served his elders and spoke only to answer the questions they asked him, before going to help the girl prepare the meal. When the two of them had set the table, they left the guests to eat while they went off to get alcohol and cigarettes from the usual shop.

Her presence among these men intrigued him greatly and as soon as they found themselves alone, he enquired,

— What are you doing here, Miss?

— And you?

— No, please. Answer me first!

— This is my place, here.

— How do you mean?

— This is where I live.

— Ah, so you're the old man's daughter.

— No. I'm with him.

— What do you mean?

— He's my old man.

— That's what I just said.

— No, he's my man.

— Ah, you live with him.

— We live as man and wife.

— How can that be?

— I can't do without him.

— It's not true love, though, is it?

— I don't know if its love but I'm crazy about him. I guess he's gotten under my skin.

— Is he the first?

— Yes, but I've been with a whole bunch of other guys since I've been with him.

— Is he the one offering you to them?

— Yes.

— And do you like it?

— I like it that he likes it.

— So, you're his slave.

— Maybe. But I need him too much.

— It's your body crying out for him. Not your heart.

— I can't manage to separate these things out.

— He makes sure you can't!

— What should I do?

— Take off.

— Who with?

— With me, of course.

— Where to?

— My place, back home in the *tribu*. I'm going tomorrow.

— So you can really take me with you?

— If you want to. It's your decision, mademoiselle.

— You sure? Not making fun of me, are you?

— What do you think?

— I think I can believe you.

— OK. Let's take back the drinks and then take off.

— No. Let's don't go back. Let's just leave now.

— It's your decision, Mademoiselle.

— OK, sir. In that case we're outa here,

The pair enjoyed their new-found intimacy and the trick they were playing on those old Romeos waiting to have a go at her under the hidden eye of the lover, concealed behind the curtains. They joked about the situation as they walked towards the little shop to call a taxi. The couple who kept the shop knew everyone in the area and had developed a soft spot for Léna, so when they saw her, both of them were in agreement. As the old man rang the taxi, the woman whispered to Léna, 'Now there's a good match for you, my girl, go on, take him and run for it!'

Chapter 6 – Tom

The taxi dropped them at Éva's, where Léna knew she would find a corner where she could sleep with her friend. She told Éva about what they had decided to do and asked her if she would perform a healing ceremony the following morning. Under Éva's care, Léna would bathe and fast, then drink a potion of bark and leaves, to help exorcise her of her demon. Late in the night, she was woken by a nightmare. She had given birth beside the sea. Then she saw her old lover floating in the belly of a giant shark as if it were a canoe. He was covered in blood and carrying off her baby. 'You dirty slut!' he sneered, 'I'm going to punish you. I'm going to give them your son to devour.' Even though she held on tightly to the young man sleeping soundly beside her, she found it hard to get back to sleep again.

At dawn, she described her bad dream to Éva, who pointed to the young man and asked her,

— Where did he find you?

— Does it matter?

— That's one of the things I have to be sure about so I can heal you better.

— It's hard to say.

— He took you away from the man in your dream.

— How do you know that?

— Your dream says it.

— Okay, so can you cure me?

— Yes, and him too, when he wakes up.

— Is that necessary?

— O yes, very much so! Old Tom is furious with both of you.

— But, apart from you, no one knows I'm here with you.

— Old Tom knows.

— Do you know him?

— Like the back of my hand. I was with him, a long time ago.

— And what was it like between the two of you?

— True love. We were very young.

— Why did you break up with him?

— He was driving me crazy.

— How?

— I was mad about him. Mad crazy about everything he did to me. Mad crazy with love and jealousy. Completely and utterly mad crazy.

— But what was he doing to you?

— Oh, you couldn't begin to imagine everything he managed to do to me!

— Yes I can! Threesomes or more in the wreck, or in the street, or maybe at the movies or inside a church. Him playing the voyeur while he sells you to drunkards. Or maybe swapping you for a chunk of venison during a card game.

— And you liked it.

— I was his slave.

— I was his slave, too.

— But you took off.

— No, he took off with someone else, a very beautiful woman, like you. She was as beautiful as her mother, who also became his mistress.

— That was my aunt and my grandmother.

— I know. Your grandmother died and your aunt took refuge in a religious sect.

— Because he was cheating on her with another aunt.

— Who he left when he tasted you.

— Am I the forbidden fruit, then?

— You are his forbidden fruit.

— Stop, you're making me cry.

— You are his forbidden fruit and he wants to keep eating you up.

— There are plenty of other women. He'll find lots more on every street corner.

— You are the fruit he bit into when it was very small, on the black stone of the graveyard of canoes.

Léna stood up and ran out of the room and down toward the mangrove swamp. Éva followed her and found her sitting in the water, under the trees crying. 'I want to die, I want to die' she sobbed brokenly. The other woman took her by the shoulders, caressed her hair and kissed her. 'Cry, go on, cry, my darling! Let all the tears in your body flow into the tide and they will carry away your pain!' In the cool of the early morning, with Léna clinging to her as if to a life-line, Éva made love to her like a fish in water; like two mutinous slaves, locked together in ecstasy. After they were spent, they searched out the bark and the leaves of medicinal plants to heal their wounds. They filled a little basin with the green liquid from the pulped plants to drink and to use to wash and rub themselves up and down with, under the outside shower. Themselves, each other and their new companion too. So long and so well did they rub him that his legs turned to cotton wool and he too was completely spent but in harmony with his body and the inner peace he was feeling for the first time ever. 'When your son is born, name him Tom, so as not to anger the fathers and grandfathers', Éva advised Léna as they were about to leave. Happy about this new start, she agreed, as she would have agreed to anything Éva wanted.

Other discussions and scenes from those few hours with Éva would only come back clearly to her later on, during the long bus journey to the *tribu*. Éva saying to her,

— You must leave today; we are too close to him here. Because he'll come looking for you as soon as he's sure you are here.

— I'll refuse to go back with him.

— He's very powerful and you've got him under your skin.

— Yes, but you're healing me; you'll get him out of me.

— You can't be sure of that until you've faced him.

— But, I'm sure of it.

— We can never be sure when it comes to a servitude that has killed a good number of us women.

— The slavery of pleasure.

— Pleasure makes you a slave to a man, my girl!

— It's the same for men, too.

— Yes, but once he has enjoyed you, girl, he moves on to something else.

— But we women can do the same if we want to.

— Woman is the bearer of children.

— But she's not obliged to keep them or to raise them.

— A child is part of a woman.

— Even if she doesn't want it?

— Whether she wants it or not, woman is the bearer of children. It's her responsibility. Women are responsible for life. That's their glory and their burden.

— Yes, but there are loads of women who abandon their kids. The world's full of deserted children who never asked to be born.

— In any event, she's the one who carries them inside her. Always. No matter what else she does or whatever she suffers before and after.

— Meaning?

— You don't get rid of a child with impunity.

— You're sounding just like him, in the dream I had last night.

She also remembered that during the healing ceremony in the shower, Éva had kept saying to her,

— You belong to him because he took you when you were little, on the rock in the graveyard of canoes.

— No! No! No!

102

— And then he let you grow up until the day he submitted you to his will again and made you his thing.

— No, No, he didn't.

— Yes, yes, he did. But I'm going to get rid of him – purge you of him.

And kneeling in front of Léna, her mouth green with chewed leaves, she had showered her with them, as Léna moaned with pleasure. Léna had finally accepted the naked truth that the healer was forcing her to admit. After sprinkling medicinal green water all over her, Éva had dried her from head to foot and comforted her. 'Yes, go on and cry, little woman, it'll do you good. I have to tear out everything that is buried inside of you and causing you all this pain, ever since it first started my child.'

She had murmured a few more words of incantation in her own language and given Léna the rest of the liquid to drink before laying down a few rules to be followed, particularly rules for when one is pregnant. Léna was convinced that with this potion, Éva would neutralise the adverse effects of anything the fisherman might have fed to her in order to increase her bondage and his possession of her.

She felt as if a burden had been lifted from her and she didn't know how to thank Éva, for she had come to her empty-handed. She helped her with all the daily chores, beginning with the dishes and the house-cleaning and sweeping the little courtyard that separated the hut from a thicket of mimosas on the slope that led down to the mangrove. She followed when Éva handed her an old jute sack and suggested going to look for a few crabs. Éva reminded her the crabs were only for her partner and said that, on this occasion, she would not eat them either, to help Léna observe the ban on salty foods and shell-fish that would make her pregnancy safer. If this was a trial, the young woman was ready to undergo it. In fact, she would gladly undergo as many trials as it took to get her out of the net in which the fisherman had caught her on that distant afternoon of her violated childhood, on the black rock of the wreck of the great canoe.

She went into the mangroves behind Éva as into an enchanted forest where her fairy godmother would wash away the bad memories of her past, and sluice them far away on the tide. Alone under the mangrove trees, they rediscovered the soothing age-old rituals of crab-fishing. Those that they found attempting to hide between two rays of sunshine finished up inside the jute bag. The thought went through Léna's mind that these crabs would end up in the cooking-pot like the crab in the old story from oral tradition. Because he keeps coming inside to cadge bits of Tado's dinner, Crab, in the story, finally finishes up inside the cooking-pot himself. She mentioned this to Éva, who replied that the crab in the story behaved just like the fisherman had towards her, but that he was still too powerful to finish up in their pot. As Léna looked doubtful, she told her he was an ogre and, although the church had put an end to the cannibalism of the ancestors, the ancestors had taught their descendants how to continue to respect the original pact that links their descendants to them, by adapting ritual practices. She added that the pact always required sacrifice, for it is through blood that the ancestors transmit once and for all what we retain of them. She ended by explaining why sorcerers and witches still exist and are still practising.

Feeling now that she could go even further with her, Léna asked some of the questions that had been nagging at her since the healing Éva had carried out.

— Can people really be cured of wanting something they feel they can't live without?

— Yes, if a person really wants to.

— I liked everything he did to me.

— Because he made you like it.

— I liked everything he made me do with the others.

— In that case, you'll like it with your new friend there as well.

— I know it's not the same with him.

— Of course, but at the end of the day, between a man and a woman, it's always the same thing. Of course he's younger and he won't give you as much as the other one did but you won't ask as much either.

— I don't know about that.

— I do. Because you will quickly fall pregnant.

— Because of everything you've given me?

— No. Because of the fisherman.

— But I've never been pregnant to him.

— You're the one who says so. He did whatever he wanted with your belly and all the rest of you at that.

— He said he had done everything possible to make sure I didn't get pregnant.

— He might have said that, but for him, it wasn't totally out of the question that you would get pregnant because that's also a way of keeping you. And this young man arrived at exactly the right time. Yes. Exactly right.

— But it is true that pregnancy is a condition you don't know anything about yet and it wouldn't have crossed your mind.

— Perhaps it's the same for all young girls with their first love.

— You're dead right, it is. They all dream of getting pregnant to their lover, of course they do! But between you and this man, it was purely and simply a rape that then gave him the power to make you his sexual object. You were nothing more than his plaything and his slave.

— I know now that it had nothing to do with love. But all the things he did to me ended up convincing me the opposite was true.

— That's the whole perversity of sexual possession. But pleasure can also be given freely. Without constraint or possession.

— People confuse love and pleasure.

— The two can go hand in hand when you really love someone.

— I'll see what happens with this boyfriend.

— It will happen and you will have a son. I'm asking you now, beforehand, to call him Tom in memory of my Tom.

— Where is he?

— Sleeping here inside me, as he was when I was expecting him.

— Did you lose him a long time ago?

— I couldn't tell you because the person I used to be passed away with him. As if my life had stopped, too.

— What was wrong with him?

— He had a bad cough that carried him off within a week.

— Was he your first son?

— The first and the last.

— Were you married to his father?

— Yes, it was a big wedding and the whole *tribu* drank, ate and danced to celebrate it. We had all the words of the old people to encourage us in our hopes and all our plans as a new couple. As for me, I was realising a childhood dream with the young man I had been in love with since school.

— So, he was your first love?

— The first and the last of its kind.

— Did he go away, too?

— No, I'm the one who left. He is still at home up there in our *tribu*. He started to drink and then he wasn't the person I had loved any more. It was death that took what we had been away from us.

— I'm sorry, it's rude of me to ask questions like this that remind you of what you have suffered.

— You have suffered worse than me, my girl, with the man you've just left. But you will find a way out because you accept what life brings. Pain and suffering doesn't weigh on you. It slides off you like water on a taro leaf.

— Perhaps I don't want to show I'm hurting.

— No. With the upbringing we are given, we can't show it. You are supposed to keep your feelings to yourself and blend into the group for the common good. You manage to do that without any difficulty. I don't. That's why I left the *tribu*. So that I could take sole responsibility for what I've chosen to become.

To the sound of the water ebbing and flowing against the roots of the mangrove trees they left, walking in single file up the path leading to Éva's field to dig some manioc. Léna vaguely remembered fishing for crabs and collecting small cockles in the mud, at low tide with her grandmother, in the distant days of her childhood, back in the *tribu*. Just as her thoughts began to drift toward the graveyard of canoes, she stopped in wonder to admire the sudden beauty of the green field. Hidden by a copse of mimosas and just now revealed, it had caught her by surprise.

Twining around their stakes, rising above the crescent-shaped mounds of earth, yam stems presented the varied green and violet tones of their heart-shaped leaves to the sun. Further down, the leaves of well-rooted taro plants opened out into great sheaves of greenery. Beside them, the leaves of the *manioc* plants branched out on their rose-coloured supports and, nearby, sweet potatoes covered a square patch of earth with more heart-shaped green leaves. A few *ambrevade* peas lent a little of their shade to lettuces, carrots, and shallots. Here and there, an occasional leafy green *brède* was growing up between yellow, bell-shaped pumpkin flowers.

— This is heaven, the young girl murmured, sitting down on an old mat in the shade of a false pepper tree.

— Yes, this is my Garden of Eden, my little piece of the Promised Land, Éva quipped.

— Everything feels so good here! And so far away from town!

— Wherever you can touch the soil and grow a plant in it, even in a pot on an apartment balcony, you can find what you are looking for in yourself.

— I think I don't know yet what I'm looking for.

— But you do know where you come from.

— Yes. Your garden reminds me of my grandmother's garden on the mountain above the sea up there in the *tribu*. From the time I was very little, she would let me rest there, on an old mat like this one, in the shade of the bois noirs in flower, while she tended the fire under a little three-legged cooking-pot.

— Wherever you go, you carry the paradise of your childhood within you.

— I would brush the yellow flowers of the bois noirs back and forth across my cheeks and under my nose to enjoy their scent.

— There are places and smells that stay with us.

— There are also places one wants to leave.

— I'll help you to leave them one day.

— I'm sure you will. When we both come back to this place.

— When you come back alone, without him.

— Today, I'm happy to follow him anywhere.

— Yes, even into someone else's arms. But, first of all, don't forget to give your son the same name as mine, as I asked you.

— Seeing as you're asking me to, I will. But if I return here alone, it will mean something has happened.

— Yes, there are things in life you can't avoid.

— Can you really not avoid them?

— Some of them, yes, others, no.

— How did you manage?

— I did the best I could. I chose to keep my dignity and the links with my own people. I was careful to preserve mutual respect and the same values of sharing and solidarity.

— How can we maintain links with our people when life separates us from them?

— We are linked by the name of the land that bears us and that we bear in turn.

— Even when we live alone far from our home and far from our own people?

— Our country's so small, we always manage to find one another. Look at the two of us, now! We hardly know each other but you came here because you knew my door was open. And it will be even more open to you from today on.

— I don't know how to thank you. I feel so dirty in front of you.

— It's the world of men that's like that, not you. That's how it functions. He possesses you, he buys you and he gets you to submit to him, the better to dominate you and do whatever he likes with you.

— And I liked it. I found my pleasure in it. And so did he, even more so, he got off on selling me and prostituting me to everyone so he could establish his power over me even more. And if he came to call me back, right here and now, maybe I'd go following after him again like a bitch in heat, Léna said in tears.

108

— No. Don't cry. He won't come looking for you here. I've undone the bonds that chained you to him. As I told you, he violated you and chained your belly in order to exert his power over you any time he wished, whenever, whatever he wanted.

— Why did none of the female relatives or the women I was staying with say anything to me?

— They were afraid of him and didn't dare get involved with what was happening to you.

— Once, I came back from the shops and found him on top of a cousin whose house we were staying at, on the very mattress she had given us. He pulled me toward them and we did it every which way as if we had the devil in us. At one point, he ordered us to do everything we could, between women, to give each other pleasure.

— And what did you do? asked Éva, her gaze suddenly penetrating.

— Something like this, she whispered, running her fingers lightly along the hem of the other's dress and lifting it up.

— That's right, yes, show me! Éva said, lying her down on the mat in the shade of the false pepper tree. And there, for the two women, time stopped still.

— When they went to get up, Éva told her, 'I will be waiting for you here, in the paradise of women, when you're tired and weary from the violence of men'.

The young woman wasn't quite the same when they rejoined her friend, who was amazed to see them so cheerful. They did the cooking, drinking an aperitif as they did so as if to seal their new intimacy. They drank wine with the meal and when he fell into the sleep of the righteous, on a mat in the shady courtyard, they stole into the bedroom and made love in silence together on the concrete floor in the sticky heat of the afternoon. In the evening, they went to bed early, because the couple were planning to leave by bus early in the morning of the following day. Then, when they heard the man snoring, they went outside hand–in–hand, to roll around entwined on the grass and on the naked earth. They spent the night there locked together, giving one another the remaining energy of their yearning bodies and their wounded beings, to gain the strength to confront the dawning day and see the future differently. At dawn, when the young man was getting into the taxi taking them to the bus station, Éva murmured to Léna as she kissed her, 'I will always be waiting for you, here in the paradise of women'.

In the *tribu*, once school began again, the relations helped the couple to settle in and get their bearings. With a cousin to help her in the house, Léna let herself be carried along by the simple pleasure of living. Trusting that Éva had prepared her womb well for the birth of her son, she experienced the period of her pregnancy as a time of exceptional grace that life was granting her. She believed nothing better could happen to her – for the sky of her childhood that she would gaze up at as she sat on her grandmother's old mat, in the shade of the bois noirs, had taken her back under its protection. She was completely happy, swimming in the waterhole, at the base of the waterfall. As it washed away the traces of the scars and lashes of a time now over, the water carried away the violence of the past.

In the hands of the old midwife, the birth was an easy one, and Tom, a beautiful baby of almost three kilos, was the object of his two mothers' single-minded attention – to say nothing of the care given to him by other relatives, from the young girls to the older women. Spoiled at home by his son and his two mothers, the happy father threw himself with enthusiasm into his teaching work, more especially because he was home, working with his own *tribu*. After school, he relaxed by playing soccer with the football team, for which he was the coach. From time to time, they went down to the village, mainly to get out a bit, buy provisions, and bring back something to spoil the baby and the mother. Sometimes, they would come back with a few young people or older men, all completely drunk, singing *tapéras* at the top of their voices. In this farthest valley up in the central mountain chain, it was a competition to see who could make the greatest use of his vocal cords in the local language, to give honour to the glory of God or the word of Christ – between the jolts from the ruts in the gravel road. (Despite the fact that, initially, the

110

idea behind *tapéras*, temperance to be exact, was part of the local Christian pact in the fight against alcoholism.)

For their part, the two young women set up a domestic routine, mothering their beautiful baby, doing the housework and the dishes or washing the nappies. They fetched wood, cooked, cut back the bush, planted flowers, pulled out weeds or went to work the taro gardens with everything necessary to make baby comfortable – his bottle, a pandanus mat and a *manou* cloth. It was also a time of long midday siestas or gossip sessions with the older women, weaving mats and baskets under the shade of the mango trees. In the arms of his mothers, aunts and grandmothers, their son, like the other children, was becoming the son of all the women present. And so Tom was growing, day by day, in their footsteps.

One morning, after they'd finished working in the fields and had been for a bathe in the waterhole, the two young women followed the creek to go fishing for shrimp, leaving the child with the others. In doing so, Léna came to discover the most paradisiacal places of the forest, be-jewelled with their mosses and ferns. And wherever they could, they would dive into the water and swim, laughing and splashing wildly like two water nymphs. Until the moment when, in their carefree solitude, hidden away from everyone and everything, the bed of the river, the current, the shore, a stone or a rock came to serve as a bed on which to discover those hidden recesses in each other's bodies, where their women's needs and desires lay dormant. There ensued a wild explosion of the desire contained too long in their young bodies, and they sought out whatever could bind them together more closely. But it was Léna, who, because of her experience with her old lover in the *tribu* and in the town, initiated the younger woman into her own ritual of pleasure. She realised then that she would not be staying around there much longer but would be constantly drawn back to Éva, to the paradise of women.

In her final months, with the strength of this conviction, Léna passed from the arms of her male partner to those of their common female companion, since she had finally succeeded in pushing them

111

into each other's arms. She already considered her to be the only mother of their son and the future wife of the happy father. Whenever she found herself alone with one or the other she began to subject them to her fantasies of what might happen between them. She reserved her afternoons for the woman and her nights for the man. She would suggest to him just what kinds of things he might like to do with her female lover, then she would wait for the right moment to take the young woman in the darkness of the thatch house, as he would later do. One afternoon, she took them both fishing for shrimp, along the creek. She led them as far as the riverbed where, after diving into a waterhole, she lay on her back, on a flat rock, opening up her body to them both. For the rest of the afternoon, she initiated her two partners into the joys of this new kind of love-making. In the evening, the teacher went down to the village with the men. He came back quite late and rather merry to find the two women together on what was going to become, for a time, their shared bed.

Having achieved her objective with this three-way connection, Léna set about strengthening it through their love-making, taking care to make sure her partner's sperm served her female lover. What had to happen did, and she became pregnant. Like an older sister, Léna initially took care of her, giving her advice on her condition and reassuring her that her own plan was to return to town. At the same time, she had the reassurance she needed on the future of her own child, Tom. If anything, the young mother-to-be loved him more than she did. Léna was a woman, a lover or a mistress, not a wife or a mother, much less a housewife. She completely lacked that inclination. She did have a predilection for pleasure and desire though. Anywhere. Any time. With anyone.

And, for the moment, the same link she had woven between the couple spurred her on to return to Éva who was waiting for her on the outskirts of the town. Just as Éva had whispered to her at the moment of her departure with the young man. It was she who had initiated Léna into love and pleasure between women. Even more than that, Léna had observed that Éva also had the knowledge and the power of women. It was an immense knowledge, as old as the world. An immeasurable power, as free as the wind. After the power men had had over her, over her body and her being, she now wanted the release promised by that immensity and that freedom with the woman who was waiting for her. It was high time she returned to Éva, to the paradise of women.

Chapter 7 – Paradise of Women

That morning, the sky was grey. Fine drizzle was moistening the grass in front of the closed door of the little hut. Sure that she would find Éva in her taro garden, Léna ran down the path between the mimosas where a few sparrows were chirping away unseen. Her heart was beating wildly, like it did when she first went running to one of her earliest rendezvous with her lover, whether in the coffee plantation, under the *niaouli* trees, beside the mangrove swamp or down at the beach. She stopped for a moment to try and get her breath back, clutching her left hand to her heart and telling herself she must be crazy. Then she remembered what Éva had told her about how she was an easy-going person who took life as it came, and continued on her way.

The garden was greener and more luxuriant than ever. In places, droplets of rain were pearling on the leaves of the yams, *ambrevades* and Kanak cabbage. On the taro leaves, they rolled into tiny transparent beads. Wearing a damp, green dress that was sticking to her body, on her knees in front of a hole she was digging with a pointed stick around a yam plant, there was Éva, in her element. Her back was turned. Léna was afraid of disturbing her and wondered if she wouldn't be better to leave. But her feet led her, despite herself, to the woman who had long been totally occupying her mind. Sensing her presence, Éva spoke, 'Is that you? I've been waiting for you. Come.' Léna went up and bent down to embrace her.

Éva let go of the digging stick to run her hands over the young woman, from her toes to her belly as if to assure herself that it really was Léna at her side. The impatience of her fingers overcame any remaining resistance and Léna abandoned herself completely to her desire. Catching a glimpse of a small patch of grey sky between two taro leaves, she let her body slide back onto the wet earth. Éva was repeating over and over how much she wanted her, begging Léna, com'on honey, give it to me. A warm liquid flowed between Éva's fingers and cupping Léna's breasts in her hands, she pressed her face hungrily against the source of her dreams. Léna's burning body contracted powerfully in a spasm and her cry mingled with the call of a heron flying above the two of them in a torrid sky where a storm was about to break.

In her turn, Léna crushed her face against Éva's belly and spurts of tangy liquid and blood flowed from her together with a stream of words that recalled those used by the fisherman to bring her to ecstasy in the wreck. And just like him, her female lover knew instinctively just how to stimulate all the most sensitive parts of her body, now in a state of complete trance. She plied her with dirty talk, with all the lewd and delicious words she knew would submit her to her total control, words she loved to hear her say when she was at the most intense point of possession. Just as, for her too, at such moments, the other became her object, her thing. Or in any event, begged for this possession as she gave in to her kisses and rhythmic caresses. Éva's body rose and fell, she cried out in a long moaning avowal of her earlier possession by the fisherman, then a final spasm left a salty taste on Léna's tongue.

Thunder growled in the distance, a few flashes of lightning appeared and then disappeared just as quickly, driven away by the amorous indifference of the two women. Despite the imminence of the storm, they knew that, right now, nothing could alter the strong bond that linked them. They knew that the splitting of their personality in the build-up to orgasm was their reliving of an earlier shared experience with the fisherman and one beyond mere sexual fantasy – since both had been his mistress some years apart.

In fact, they had met at a dance not long after Éva arrived in town, and it was he who had shown her the sources and variety of pleasurable feelings she could obtain from her body, whether alone or otherwise. Dawn would find her clinging to him in the wreck where he would subsequently be able to submit her to his every desire. And she wanted nothing more, as, feeling him inside her quickly became a daily need, even a question of survival. He played the game for a while. Acting the devoted partner, he would shower her with little gifts after the nights when he possessed her as and when he wanted. In a corridor, between two parked cars, even on the public pavement at ungodly hours. They both took so much pleasure in the risks of this game of 'hide and seek love-making' that, one night, a priest surprised them in the entrance to his church. They pretended he wasn't there and his unexpected presence pushed them to double their efforts on the hard dusty concrete floor. The fisherman had her say she was sister Éva, as in the Bible, ridden by brother Adam, debauched by a satanic snake, in the name of the Father, the Son, and the Holy Ghost. They heard the priest moan and leave them precipitously with a ruffled swish of his indignant cassock.

After that scene, Éva asked herself for the first time how far her submission would go and whether she would have done the same thing in the broad light of day. Then, she forgot about it, until another evening, when, after a bout of drinking with one of his closest fisherman friends, he wanted to push her into the friend's arms, claiming he himself was too drunk to make love to her. She realised, then, that if their relationship was going to be reduced to this, she had better leave him before he handed her over, bound hand and foot, to all and sundry. She refused his proposal, even although, at that stage, she was finding it hard to see clearly because of the constant need for him eating away at her at every moment. Even in the happiest times of a former life, with her husband, she had never felt a craving and an absence in herself whose urgency could be satisfied by only one man in the world. And his mere presence made her see the world differently. So she spent most of her time with him, neither wanting nor asking for anything more, no longer worrying about the future.

And then, one Saturday morning, they went as they usually did to the boat shop, so named for the pictures from maritime history above the glass counter that contained a very fine collection of miniature yachts. There they met a cousin of the fisherman's, with Maria, his companion, a woman with a dazzling smile and full of joie de vivre. She laughed at anything and everything but, when required, was also adept at women's tasks, from weaving to cooking and even to working the fields, skills she had learned from her mother and relations back in the *tribu*.

She had run away to town, a few years back, with a suitor her family wouldn't have a bar of because he was the son of the Javanese 'of' one of the settlers of the area. The indentured labourers were given the name of 'the Javanese of' followed by the French family name of the settler, or the Kanak name for the locality, a name recalling its traditional topography. And this expression, 'the Javanese of', had the meaning of 'the slave of', for the Kanak knew full well that Indonesian, Indochinese or Tonkinese labour had been imported by the French colonial administration to do the work that they, as men and women of the land, refused to do. However, love and youth cared not a whit for traditions and prejudices and the couple had decided to run away to town where they could love each other freely. So freely did they love that, after a certain period of time, they ended up separating. Both went their separate ways and so Maria found herself with the cousin of the fisherman whom they had met with his companion, Éva, that fateful morning, in the boat shop.

The little wooden colonial house in which the shop was situated had just been repainted by the young owners; a couple who were the target of all the scandalmongers of the colony. Widely rumoured to be the natural daughter of her lover, the woman had also become the partner of his son, to the hurt pride of their common genitor, who had committed suicide. The mother, who now considered herself vindicated for her husband's multiple betrayals, offered them the boat shop before going back to the bush to consign herself to oblivion. And the regulars of the shop didn't fail to regale new customers with the story. In this way, it became a weird kind of 'reverse' advertising for all those who frequented the area.

Subjugated by Maria, Éva drank in her words while, under the mango tree, she told her the story that she herself had heard many times. The two men joined them and they took the path that led to their hut near the wreck, by the sea. While she was cooking a yam and a few taro from a *pola* basket left there by a visiting female cousin, the men went a little further down the beach to throw out a net.

They brought back some picot fish that the women quickly put on the grill to cook. They then set the pieces of yam and taro in coconut milk on an enamel dish decorated with red roses. Éva took the dish and Maria carried a big mat of woven pandanus, with a basket containing the plates and utensils, covered by a multicoloured Uvéa[21] cloth, over to a big *bourao* tree[22] situated a little further away, under which they liked to eat, to rest or picnic with the fisherman and their friends when it was too hot. The two men followed with the wine and the guitar from the house, to liven up a sunny afternoon that looked full of promise.

The meal was a long and lingering affair, with discussions between the two men on the two new associations set up in the *tribus* by the Catholic and Protestant churches to defend the rights of the first inhabitants of the country, the indigenous peoples; the latest news of the family; and lots of laughter well washed down with red wine. A little later, high tide was a pretext for casting the nets again and grilling more picots, followed by a splash in the lagoon. They recalled

21 A piece of material with Oceanian motifs (Transl.)
22 *Hibiscus tiliaceus.*

one fishing expedition for *trocas*,[23] when the men competed with the women to see how long they could hold their breath, drawing the consonants of their family names with pieces of coral on the sand as deep down as possible. One fisherman was renowned for having always been the winner of this competition – that is, until the day he was beaten by a woman.

They were full of the pleasure of being together, carried along on the music that the fisherman was playing on his guitar. The other three sang along as he strummed effortlessly, playing a repertoire of Melanesian and Polynesian tunes, and refrains from popular songs and hymns. With the same extraordinary inspiration, he could string together the notes of countless tunes: *Mes amis la vie est belle, Vaya con dios, La paloma, La mer, Je chante une romance, La vie en rose, Le Temps des cerises*, the words of the song from the Loyalty Island of Maré, *Nengone*,[24] or *Olé, olé, tëu*[25] –or the hymn, *Wëgo nî co caa*.[26] When he held his guitar close to him like a sweetheart, the country's entire repertoire flowed through his fingers. His virtuosity amazed everyone, connoisseurs and amateurs alike, and whenever anyone questioned him about it, he would answer that he had taught himself. A *popwaalé* once told him that he drew plaints and sighs and cries from his instrument, as if he were making love to it. He found the comparison so unexpected that it sent him into a fit of laughing. The European added, just as seriously, that it was the first time he had heard a self-taught guitarist who reminded him of Django Reinhardt, Narciso Yepes, Compay Segundo or Manitas de Plata. When he asked him if he had heard of these famous virtuosos, the fisherman replied that the only guitar-playing he had ever heard was in the film *Forbidden Games*.

Intoxicated on wine, love, sunshine, sea, music and laughter, everyone took turns strumming the guitar while the others danced.

---

23 *Trochus niloticus*. (Transl.)
24 Name of the island of Maré and famous song. (Transl.)
25 "Thank you, thank you to the pair of you" song. (Transl.)
26 "Here I am, Father" hymn (Transl.)

Waltz and tango, two-step and rock-and-roll, Charleston and cha-cha-cha, Tahitian *tamuré* and the *cap*.[27] At the end of the afternoon, the cousin ended up snoring on a corner of the mat. The other three went on joking, laughing, and singing. And at one point, Maria collapsed onto her back laughing uncontrollably. Still laughing, she found herself with her head against the fisherman's chest and was suddenly still. Equally intoxicated, Éva joined the couple.

And so she broke down the barriers they had put up for themselves against the fisherman. Up until then, she had clung to the idea that she would have left him rather than give herself to another man whenever he ordered her to. Even if she often pretended to while they were playing out their wildest fantasies together. But, as with him, with Maria, the attraction was fatal. Given the intensity of the life force that flowed in the young woman and the passion she excited, it could hardly be different. It was then that Éva discovered that she could love a woman.

Until then, all she knew about lesbians came from the few pictures she had seen lying around in the house of one of her *popwaalé* bosses, who was one herself. Sometimes she served her boss and her lovers their morning coffee in her boss's big bed. On one occasion, she came upon them inadvertently on the big living room rug, but got out of there so fast they barely had time to register her presence. And later, when the husband asked her if she had noticed anything equivocal about Madame's relationship with her friends, she had asked him in her turn:

— Please, Monsieur. What do you mean by 'equivocal'?

— I mean bizarre.

— Bizarre? What do you mean by bizarre?

— Did I say bizarre? How bizarre!

— Now it's Monsieur who's being bizarre.

— Non, that's not it, Éva! That line comes from a famous film.

— Ah? It's the title of a film, is it? That's bizarre because I haven't seen it advertised at the cinema.

27 A dance from the Loyalty Islands (Transl.)

120

— Non, it's a game. Like the one Madame is playing with her friends behind my back.

— What's the name of this game Madame is playing at with her friends behind your back, sir?

— They're playing strip jack naked.

— Ah, so they're just playing?

— You don't think they're playing?

— No, I don't think so, Monsieur.

— Ah thank you, Éva. I can't tell you how much of a relief that is. How much reassurance you've given me.

— Really? Well, if Monsieur feels relieved, that's a good thing.

— What do you mean, Éva, 'if Monsieur feels relieved...' My honour and my virility are at stake here.

— Your what, Monsieur?

— My virility, Éva. Monsieur's virility.

— And what's that, Monsieur?

— That's what I have in my pants, Éva.

— Oh sorry, Monsieur.

— You've no need to be sorry, Éva, as long as Madame is happy with my plaything and doesn't play up with her friends behind my back.

— No, Monsieur, she's not playing up. I mean, they're most definitely not playing.

After this exchange, Éva wondered, once more, whether she would ever really understand white people and their funny business. However, when, a little later, it was Monsieur's turn to surprise Madame and her friends in their birthday suits on the living room rug, Éva was sacked for having, as he put it, lied to Monsieur, and as she put it, for having betrayed Madame. Éva left, convinced from that time on, that she really wouldn't ever understand the ins and outs of the *popwaalé* world.

And now that she was in the same boat, or aboard the same wreck, to use her own expression, she considered that, with Maria and the fisherman, they were simply living the situation as it came, without complicating things unnecessarily. She included in this the cousin, who had chosen to close his eyes to anything and everything that might arise while he slept off his wine on the floor of the hut. It was then that the fisherman invited the two women to play at being what he called shipwreck victims in the upturned hull.

Some evenings, when the two cousins had drunk too much and fallen asleep early, the women had the whole night to themselves. And then they could harmonise their songs of love with the music of the waves, and share their unique feminine perception of everything that was happening to them and what was unfolding within them. They were alone, outlaws and illegals in the world of men, and their only margin for manoeuvre lay in this intimacy, these closeted moments, stolen from a life of daytime public submission to a male-dominated order. Only the night allowed them to enter into possession of what was forbidden them in the daylight world of men. They showered upon one another all the love they had been carrying within them since the night of ages, acutely aware that the dawn would find them back once again at the bottom of the social pile. Forgetting their age-old subjugation and subordinate status that had been legitimised time and time again, they sailed from island to island in search of their own paradise. Knowing full well that, in the morning, they would again be forced to betray their Amazon souls to the bellicose madness of men and the violence inherent in the male social pact to keep women in their place, they immersed themselves in the night's bliss. These sisters of the 'second sex', one half of the sky, the salt of the earth, were sailing the seas of sensual pleasure and ecstasy, dancing the dance of hungry bellies in a quest for something sublime that must lie beyond the derisory illusions of orgasm. From the beginning of time, their female bodies had been nothing but receptacles of male lust, the warrior's rest or the soldier's rapine. So why shouldn't they steal a bit of quality time, let their hair down and live it up a little on their own while the real thieves were sleeping the sleep of the just? With irreverent mocking humour, they would mimic the positions of their lovers on top of them, laughing like crazy women playing naughty schoolgirl pranks. They would ape the gestures of the sighing lover 'panting like a furnace', some great snow-man melting with passion like a lollipop in the sun. With cheeky irony, they would parody the slick pick-up lines of the professional *Don Juan*, parrot the spiel of the aging seducer or the macho jock. Then they would jump on their broomsticks, imitating the contortions of witches burned alive, in the name of globalisation, on the last funeral pyres of the new universal inquisition policing the dominant ideology, the single way of thinking serving the rich and powerful of the planet. Eyes wide open, they loved each other to a thousand little deaths, vowing eternal passion. Their relationship, however, had more to do with game-playing than true love. But it did occasionally allow Éva and Maria to slip away, out of the clutches of the two drunken cousins.

Clinging to Léna, under the heart-shaped leaves of the taro, in the garden, ravaged and revived by the rain storm, Éva recounted the story of her former love with Maria, letting her know in this way the nature of the relationship she wanted them to share, intense, fleeting, and free. Free of the constraints of the everyday routines that wear love away. Free of the passion and possession that alienate. Free of the jealousy and envy that poison. Outside time, endlessly, they made love to each other, in the muddy water of the ditch. Then, staggering under the force of the storm, they went down toward the mangroves to cling to each other again in the mud of the mangrove trees, under the waves of the rising tide. When they returned to the little house, they hosed themselves down in the rain. Then they drank a glass of citron and fell asleep, exhausted, on Éva's old bed, locked in each others arms. The saucy smile of Marilyn Monroe watched over them from the faded poster on the wall.

Little by little, her time with Éva enabled Léna to break free from the bondage that had been totally enslaving her body to sexual pleasure. As the days passed, the older woman led her along the paths of dream and the reading of nature. And to that other reading of the world, through its commonplace events, the minor happenings and actions of their daily lives. Then on to the other side of the real. Along the path of silence and the word. The silence that speaks and the word that is silence. The path of knowledge and wisdom. Not the path of the male holders of traditional knowledge, but the fluid, pragmatic and daily pathways that transmit the savoir-faire of women: The language of the insects and the birds and the behaviour of the shellfish on the coral flat or the crustaceans in the mangroves; the message of lizard, mullet, and eel. Such a well-spring of knowledge inherited from the island's oral traditions and conjugated in the feminine could not but undo the construction of woman as sexual object, enabling her to be reborn, freed from her internalised fantasies dominated by male orgasm. Éva compared her metamorphosis to that of the chrysalis of the cicada, emerging from the earth to fly away, singing, toward the sky. Or, more prosaically, explaining to her that, once she had washed, dressed and perfumed her body, not a trace remained of what they had been doing together on the ground, on the grass, in the field or in the mangroves.

'It's not our acts that make us dirty. It's we who make our acts unclean,' she would repeat to Léna to convince her, after lovemaking, to leave their unbridled sexuality there where it reigned triumphant. On the ground, in the mud, on the grass, against a tree or in the water. 'For it belongs to nature. You have to leave it there so as not to be too troubled by something that is quite simply a part of the world into which we are born and given senses to explore. Why so much talking, so much fuss, so many illusions around love or sex when we know that they are not eternal, just as we, and indeed, all the things of this world, are not.

'Grasp love when it comes toward you and let it leave when it wants to rather than killing it off little by little in long-term relationships like marriage, or cohabitation on the grounds of saving face, or appearances, or the children, or a few material possessions. All that has nothing to do with love; or love has already gone. Love catches you on the wing but, in the time it takes to learn to use your wings and fly away, it has already burned you up completely. Its consummation consumes you. And it's better if you are able to fly with your own wings, for it will always drop you when you least expect it. When you find that, for a long time already, just as he was before he was with you, your lover has been in another's arms.

'So live your life and your love as if you were going to lose them the next moment, like everything in this world. And protect yourself from memory as soon as it entertains the illusion of what is dead and gone. Erase it when it chains you to the past, making you forget the present and ignore the future. Don't let yourself be bogged down in pain and suffering when you still have everything to hope for from life. Don't swim against the current. The river always flows to the sea. But day follows night. And this alternation of time you see swallowing up your life from day to day is all that there is. So why cling to grass that comes out by the roots? Why continue to bite into a fruit that is rotten? Carpe diem: Live to the very fullest the love that comes along and takes flight again without taking leave!

'But should you want to choose for yourself the day you yourself take flight, or the day you take marriage vows, look twice at your love, for it can wear many faces. A smile in the morning, laughter at midday and a frown in the evening. Promises, lies and betrayal are the infernal trio of love. So, you'd better be prepared for this, rather than play the holy virgin waiting for the angel who will never arrive in a month of Sundays. For the stories of Prince Charming, of fairies and witches are only make-believe. At best, they end up with a little grandfatherly groping, at the worst, a little fatherly rape. Dads and granddads, they're the true sorcerers and ogres of the fairy stories. While she waits to be handed over with the dowry, made up, trussed-up, in a booby-trapped package posted off to the future mother-in-law – that is, if the mother-in-law is still around. Dressed-up, veiled, and shoed, led toward the chains of marriage, the reins of the wedding bridle around her neck. While in reality, babies, born of fathers undisclosed or unknown, or out of wedlock, come to swell the ranks of humiliated women.'

And that is how it was, at the time of the free union of Éva and Léna, on the edge of the town, in between doing housekeeping for the boss-lady and working their gardens under the mimosas, fishing for crabs in the mangroves, and partying at weekends with cousins of both sexes and a cohort of relatives and friends.

Chapter 8 – Léna

Éva's hut was situated at the bottom of the garden of the large residence for which she was caretaker and cleaner. The owner's house was on the heights, with a view of the sea. Her employer was an only child, a painter who spent most of her time travelling the world with her exhibitions, discovering other countries and colours to add to her palette. This gave Éva the freedom to come and go with whom she pleased and to make her house a weekend meeting place for many of the young men and women from the local area looking for music, dancing and parties. This also suited her boss, who was something of a Bohemian and who told anyone who'd listen that she'd rather see people having a good time at her house than having delinquents wanting to trash it. The nearest neighbours were more than a kilometre away, so Éva's little community was able get together as they would in any coastal *tribu*, with taro gardens, the mangroves and the sea at their back door. Love affairs blossomed, solutions to problems were found, and disputes settled. Customary ceremonies of birth, marriage and mourning were prepared and held, and every Sunday they would do a *bougna*.

Everyone who could, helped gather wood from under the mimosas, *gaiacs*, blackcurrant bushes and false pepper trees. They would set their bundles of sticks down beside the stones and *niaouli* bark for the ground oven under the three pepper trees that shaded the entrance to the track down to the gardens and the mangroves. They would stack a few logs for splitting with the axe, and hang bunches of bananas from the branches. In a thatched lean-to with woven bamboo walls, two iron bars laid across big concrete blocks supported the big cast iron cooking pots and aluminium pans over the wood fire. A jerry-can and a large glass flagon kept filled with fresh water squatted in one corner. On the other side, there were *pola* baskets and jute sacks of yams, taros, sweet potatoes and dried coconuts. Dishes, sugar, rice, and tea were stacked along shelves on the wall. Alongside them were jars of ground coffee, the aroma of which would float through the early morning air. Kitchen utensils – tea-strainers, ladles, skimmers, scrapers, frying-pans, saucepans and other small cooking pots – hung from a few nails. A few old, up-turned petrol cans and two wooden benches served as seats where you could snuggle close to the fire during the cool season. Its flames lit up long evenings of partying or mourning, where wailing alternated with singing, quarrelling and chatting. And when there was a big crowd, pandanus mats would be spread out on the beaten earth for everyone to sleep off the night's drinking and partying.

But when it was sunny, the favourite gathering place was in the shade of the three false pepper trees. On Sundays, before dawn, chickens would be plucked and fish scaled by the dim light of a kerosene lamp. Yams, taros, sweet potatoes, manioc, bananas and pumpkins would be peeled and cut into pieces. Lettuces, leafy *brèdes*, sticky Kanak cabbage, pumpkin, chinese cabbage, and chokos would be stripped and shredded. The peelings, empty shells, scraps of food, rubbish and various empty tin cans were then thrown into a hole, dug by the young men lower down the hill, well out of sight.

Then, at first light, some of the group would go down to the garden and bring back young banana leaves and vines for preparing the *bougna*. They would soften them over the fire as others lit the wood piled up on the stones to heat them. The women would choose three of the most supple and pliable banana leaves to lay on the bed of vines. They would prick the pieces of yam, taro, sweet potato and pumpkin and arrange them in a circle on the youngest banana leaf, with the chicken, or fish or *roussette* in the middle. Then they would add salt and chopped spring onions before the young men came around with the bucket of coconut milk to ladle it over the *bougna*. When it was finished, it looked like a string of little mauve or yellow-coloured islands floating on a small white lake surrounded by green slopes. At this point the women would all take great care to inspect the banana leaves for the slightest tear that might allow the precious coconut milk to seep out. If one was found, another leaf was immediately placed underneath it to prevent any leakage. Éva would sometimes joke to the young men present that the banana leaf was like the virgin who will only give her best milk after a steamy night in a hot oven. She would add that it was important to prepare her marriage bed carefully by spreading out the hot coals evenly to prevent her leaves from being burnt to a cinder.

— Such is the fate of all those – women and men – who throw themselves onto the fires of passion and shrivel up before their time, she would chuckle.

— So you better choose your leaf carefully, eh Aunty, one of them asked mischievously.

— You have to find one that hasn't got a hole in it.

— Yes, the youngest, the softest, the most pliant.

— Of course. Otherwise, how do you keep your juice in?

— I can always put another leaf underneath.

— So you're one of those who's never happy with just one, aren't you!

— Especially not if it's already got a hole in it.

— But you're probably the one that put the hole in it!

— Not necessarily. It could've been someone else.

— *If it is not thee, then 'tis thy brother.*

— Yet, but to each his own... heart.

— You said it.

— That particular leaf is also called the heart leaf, isn't it?

— Exactly. That's why you have to protect it.

— You can't protect your heart.

— No. Let's just say, you shouldn't expose it to all weathers.

— There's always one cyclone stronger than the others that comes along and sweeps away everything in its path.

— That's the one that tears holes in the banana leaves.

— But not the heart leaf.

— That's so the banana tree can keep the best part of itself safe.

— It's also the most fragile leaf.

— Just like the human heart where life hangs on a heartbeat.

— That's why it hurts so much when you get heart trouble.

— Especially the first time. Afterwards, you try to develop a resistance.

— We're big boys and girls now, we've been immunised. There's no need to suffer from heart trouble.

— Well, that's what people think.

— It's better that way though, isn't it Aunty?

— It's better to know what we are.

— So what are we, then?

— Just a breath of air.

— Not just that, though, Aunty?

— Well, that's what they call us when we die and they take the bunch of cordyline to the maternal uncles as a sign to come and take us back home.

— We're only a breath of air.

— It takes your breath away, doesn't it?

— Yeah, Aunty, sure does. Takes my breath away.

— Get away! If it really took your breath away, you wouldn't still be of this world now, would, you?

— Ah, you've always got the right answer, Aunty. Always teaching us, showing us the funny side. That's why we all love you so much.

— Good. That way there'll be lots of you to accompany me to my final dwelling-place, the day I leave you.

— Anyway, lots more water will have flowed under our bridges before then, Aunty.

Éva would laugh and joke like this with the young men as they moved between the women to ladle the coconut milk over the *bougnas* or brought long sticks to spread out the hot stones and the coals for the ground oven. The women joked with them too as they gently folded the banana leaves over the food dowsed in coconut milk. Once they were closed and tied up, the *bougnas* were placed side by side next to the oven like so many green parcels. While one person placed them on the embers and the burning hot stones, another would dip his hand into a bucket and splash water over them to put out any sparks. Lastly, the women would pack pieces of taro and manioc, smaller green parcels, and banana bark around them to reduce the heat of the stones, then they'd cover the *bougnas* with the *niaouli* bark that had been piled up ready.

While the *bougnas* were cooking in the ground, they would chat, while some washed under the hose behind the woven coconut palm screen that served as a shower at the bottom of the yard. Some would go down and cast nets at the edge of the mangrove, while others drank and sang. The women would prepare the green salad or load the scraps and peelings into a wheelbarrow and wheel them down to the rubbish hole. Others would wash their clothes and spread them out to dry on the bushes and in the thickets, well out of sight, out of respect for the men. There was always a brother or a cousin among them to whom the prohibitions surrounding women's clothing applied. These get-togethers still required that certain taboos be observed, at least in broad daylight. Those (of both sexes) who did skirt the rules would take every precaution. But sometimes the liberal quantities of alcohol would release inhibitions and lead to rules being broken outright. And so, a couple wanting to be alone in the middle of the afternoon might stumble upon another pair, who should really have been under tabou, lying together under the mimosas or the false pepper trees. Even Éva hid her relationship with Léna, out of consideration for those who might be disturbed by such a breech of custom – or would be if anyone should speak of it openly. Because she also knew that silence didn't mean nobody knew.

But in this little no-man's-land, there was no need to overdo feelings of guilt. So the two women were quite relaxed and had plenty of time, when nobody else was around, to make love to one another. These weekends with the extended family and friends were most often days of joyful abstinence for them. But sometimes, a simple fluttering of the eyelashes would find them under one of their secret bushes, enjoying fleeting moments of intense, unseen pleasure, to reemerge and return to the group as if nothing had happened.

Until one day, Éva's employer caught them in her sights as she was looking through her binoculars toward the sea beyond the mangroves. Acting as the liberated woman she believed herself to be, she followed them and they ended up taking her as well, in the garden in the rain, and in the mud of the mangrove swamp. They laughed behind her back to see their hysterical boss, tethered to the trunk of a mangrove tree, her body spattered with slime, begging them for more in the rising tide. A slippery siren, she played the role of masochistic slave, on her knees in the mud, before washing the sludge off the bodies of her lovers, who were surprised by so much ardour. Exhausted, she sometimes followed Léna's example and dozed off on the grass or in the shade of the mangrove trees.

Only Éva conserved all her energy and found even more as she hunted for crabs and little shellfish. When they went to fetch firewood it was she who would cut it down with her machete and carry it on her back in a bundle tied up with straw or vines. Sometimes, she found the other two rolling around in the grass, in the mud or in the waves. And she got a kick out of clearing her throat and calling out things like, 'Hey, you two, someone's coming!' and then announcing, 'OK, it's only me! You know no one's around here during the week! Relax you crazy fools', and she would laugh at their discomforted expressions. 'Oh go on, don't look like so embarrassed, sisters, you've still got all the time in the world to roll around together before life casts us up on the shores of death like the wrecks that we are!' she would continue before going back up to the cabin, bundle of wood on her back and machete and bag full of her catch in her hand. On the path, she would think to herself that the flesh was weak and that, personally, she preferred her freedom to its bondage. And when the other two took their time coming back, she knew that sensual pleasure was once again locking them together in a carnal prison. Sensual pleasure she had come to think was only an illusion that illustrated the brevity of all the things of this life. At the same time, she freely admitted that, for certain people, giving it up meant taking all the savour out of life. But she herself refused to be a slave to it. Certainly not. Especially as she considered that the loss of self caused by the grip of passion was an alienation akin to the sorcerer's enslavement of his victim.

She didn't want to be playing this cat-and-mouse game with Léna nor with her boss nor with anyone else. Even if there was a flattering inversion of roles, with Madame begging for the whip or the cane, it was only a passing game. Everyone would soon revert to their real status of master, servant or mistress. Minus the word-plays and all jokes aside. And still, nothing could replace within her the lost bond with her dead son. That was beyond love, memory and time.

Before flying off again to other climes, the boss spent her last nights wearing only a mask, on all fours between Éva and Léna, who pretended to be her jailors. Sometimes they were on the verge of hysterical laughter at the rather grotesque postures of Madame as she begged continually to be beaten or punished, but they played along, well aware of the real sadism of the domination exerted by most of their bosses. They realised that they had mostly enjoyed the time spent with her on her rather comical little perversions.

During the day, she painted them a lot, not their love life at all but rather scenes from their daily life. The vibrant colours of their flower-patterned mission dresses glowed bright against the luminous skies of the island in portraits of groups of women sitting preparing the *bougna*. Éva's inspired face, smiling as if she was recalling a distant memory, often dominated the rest of the painting so that she seemed to be the only person in it. The artist tried to capture the serenity Éva carried within her beneath her laughing exterior and rather brusque manner. And her model was grateful to the artist for representing her in this way. This, too, confirmed for her that Madame was decidedly unlike the others. On the day of her departure, she offered Éva her favorite painting. It was the one with Éva, standing out on the coral flat at daybreak, a lone seagull in front of her, as she looked out toward the horizon as if toward a new life.

Around the same time, Maria abandoned the fisherman's cousin for one of the young men she had met at Éva's. Éva understood immediately from the way they behaved toward one another that their relationship could last quite some time, and she took them under her protective wing. They came to see her often, like children of the house, and helped with the daily chores. The garden quickly became their favorite place.

They cut back the mimosas, the false pepper trees and weeds, and piled up and burned the resultant debris to clean up the space to be cultivated. With pick and crowbar they broke up the soil and turned it over. They raked the earth into square plots and threw up the yam mounds using spade and hoe, digging wide ditches around the beds for irrigation. They burned stumps and pulled them out by the roots to clear more space for planting.

They brought back plants and seedlings from the store, from the *tribu* or the outskirts of the city. They filled bags and baskets with anything they could plant. Nimble feet carried yam heads, banana shoots, sprouting sweet potatoes, cuttings of manioc and taro to the garden to be planted. All of the cuttings were heeled straight into the ground, but they waited patiently for the soil to be exactly right before planting the yams into the holes marked by wooden stakes. They took the time to hunt out or exchange different varieties with relations or friends, and they always put aside any rare or new plants for the garden they were tending with Éva. It was a way of thanking her for her affection and motherly protection. Because they were working so closely together, Éva soon detected in Maria's face the earliest signs of the mother-to-be. She advised her to avoid heavy work in the taro garden from then on and asked Léna to take good care of her.

Maria settled for looking after the house-garden. She began by collecting the small branches of hibiscus or bougainvillea that Léna pruned with the secateurs from the hedge separating them from the boss lady's big yard, and putting them in the ground at the four corners of the cabin. She hoed and turned the dry soil between the dahlias and the gerberas that had been wilting against the walls. She planted out pieces of American border hedge all around the cabin. She sowed nasturtiums, French marigolds, and impatiens between clusters of crimson purslane.

She set about breaking up the clods of earth between the circle of stones she placed on both sides of the path leading to the taro garden and the mangroves. In the turned soil between the *coleus* and *cordyline* bushes she planted citronella. She got the ancestral lawn beneath the false peppertrees to grow again and helped it along by pulling out the weeds as they emerged from day to day.

Maria avoided thinking about her recent past and focused rather on memories of childhood years spent with her paternal grandmother. At that time, she and her widowed grandmother had lived with an old settler, once he himself became a widower. At the end of their lives, the old couple had thus sealed their first love, earlier forbidden by colonial apartheid. They had been forced apart, to live each in his and her own separate camp and had let themselves be carried along by existence and the obligations and duties of their respective universes. Little by little, time overtook that world and they found themselves together again at the twilight of their lives.

Maria knew nothing about all that until, one day, when her lover, the son of an Indonesian indentured labourer, suggested she go and ask the old settler for a horse he wanted to ride to round up the cattle,

— You're his favorite granddaughter, he'll say yes straight away.

135

— Cut it out! You know he lives with my grandmother but I'm not his granddaughter.

— That's your story.

— What d'ya mean?

— I'm just repeating what everyone says.

— What's that?

— Nothing, I didn't say a thing. Sorry.

— Sorry for what? I want to know what everyone says!

— No, I was just being smart, that's all. I'm like you; I don't know a thing.

— Yes you do. So just tell me right now what everyone says or I'll go straight to my grandmother and ask her.

— I can't tell you. I don't have the right.

— But if it's what everyone says!

— I didn't know you didn't know.

— Well, now you do know, you have to tell me.

— How can I put it... well... everyone says you're their granddaughter, of the two of them, that is.

— He's my father's father?

— Yes, they've been in love forever. Since they were little. They grew up together with my grandfather. He was the go-between for their rendezvous. Once he even took a beating, got horse-whipped, rather than betray them. That was to protect her because he was in love with her too. He loved her till his deathbed when I heard him saying her name over and over. 'Forgive me Maria, I'm so, so sorry!' and she turned her head away to hide her tears.

But she didn't dare ask her grandmother until one afternoon when she surprised her standing in front of a framed photo of the settler's legitimate daughter in riding clothes.

— The spitting image of her mother, just as you're the spitting image of me.

— What was she like to you, grandmother?

— She didn't know me.

— And her mother.

136

— The same.

— But you knew them both well.

— Better than anyone. And I could recount their whole lives on this property, day by day. I knew every little thing they did and said.

— Until their car accident.

— She wanted to go out one night, just she and her daughter, even though she barely knew how to drive. They were coming home. Their bodies were found on either side of the car, which was a total wreck. And on the ground next to the daughter, there was a little red and black rosette from the party they'd been to.

— And you consoled grandpa.

— He already had me, even before I had your father. Well before his wife and daughter. I was always his.

— So papa is really his son?

— Yes, and I'm happy to be able to tell you this at last. It takes a weight off my shoulders.

— And papa, did you tell him, too?

— Your father is the oldest son of my mother's clan. He carries its name, the name he gave to you. It's the family that protected me, who raised your father and made a man of him. And in return, his sons and his brothers gave life back to a clan that was dying out, with only my uncle and father-in-law as its last descendants.

— But didn't you tell papa?

— And what about you, my grand-daughter, are you going to tell him now that you know everything?

— No, I can't.

— You see what I mean.

— But why, grandmother, why?

— Well, why aren't you going to tell your father everything I've just told you?

— Why not? To protect myself.

— Yes, be wary of words that can be turned against you.

Sitting in the shade of the false pepper trees, by the sea, feeling the baby move inside her as the days went by, Maria remembered the words and the teachings of her grandmother. Then, one afternoon, after siesta, her partner came to tell her that he had found work in a mining centre, out in the bush. He was leaving as soon as possible to look for somewhere to live there. A little later Maria joined him, with Léna accompanying her, on Éva's advice.

Chapter 9 – The Wreck

Tom is the first to get up at around four in the morning; he puts a pot of water on to boil while he takes his shower. Léna wakes and sets out the coffee, milk and sugar and the two teaspoons beside their two bowls. Then she pours the boiling water into the flower-patterned thermos before also going off to take her shower. As she is doing her hair in the mirror over the washbasin, she hears the sound of a large blue fly buzzing around her. Léna wonders what it can be doing there so early in the morning then goes off to join Tom for coffee.

After breakfast she washes the bowls and puts everything on the table away. Then she gets her bag ready while Tom packs the lengths of material for the wedding they are going to, in the village of Léna's second mother. This was the mother after whom she had been named, her namesake or *deviné*, considered to be her double in her own generation. Tom closes the box of stores before loading it into the car his cousin has loaned him for the occasion. Making sure they haven't left anything behind in the small studio flat, they set off at around five.

After the tollbooths, Tom turns on the radio and hears Channel K broadcasting a Bob Marley selection – *No Woman No Cry*,

Redemption Song and *Three Little Birds*. He hums along to *Everything Gonna Be Alright*, keeping time tapping his fingers on the wheel. Feeling at peace with herself and happy to be with Tom, a smiling Léna sings the words with him, clapping in time. They leave the town to this musical accompaniment in the peace of the dawning day.

On Channel K, they travel from reggae to Kanéka, from Vanuatu to Fiji, Kinshasa to La Havana, both singing along to *Te querida presencia, commandante Che Guévara*, enjoying its vibrant nostalgia before returning to Kanaky with *Olé, olé tëu*.

As day breaks through the mist and the dew, Léna remarks that she has seen a little old man on their right, waiting at the side the road. As Tom has kept on driving without taking any notice or as if he hasn't seen anything, she suggests he should have stopped as, 'perhaps the old fulla wanted to hitch a ride'.

— What old fulla?

— The one on the side of the road, dopey, over there on the right, look.

— You sure?

— I saw him as plain as day.

— Do you want to go back and check?

— Yes, but what if he's gone…

— No worries. It'll either mean you dreamt him up or you must still be half asleep. It happens, you know, when you get up early like this. Let's go back. At least that way we'll be sure.

They drive back to the spot Léna indicated but there is no one there. Tom does his best to reassure Léna, repeating that it's nothing unusual this early in the morning. She doesn't tell him she thought it was the old fisherman she had seen.

They set off again. A bird of prey on its early morning hunt circles just above them, its powerful wings cutting through the air before it passes out of their field of vision as they gather speed. On the international news, the radio announces the refusal of a number of settlers to withdraw from the Gaza strip that the Israeli army, Tashal, is evacuating on behalf of the government.

— Do you think it'll come to an end one day?

— What's that?

— That war, of course. It feels like I've been living with it ever since I was born, since I started to be able to understand the news on the radio.

— It's true we've grown up with it but there've been some pretty big changes since Sabra and Chatila, Arafat's expulsion from Beirut, the kids of the Intifada, and Palestinian autonomy.

— But aren't they still shooting at each other?

— The peace process is a long one because it's been a long war. You have to see this withdrawal positively as a victory negotiated between the two countries and their foreign allies.

— So it's peace that puts an end to warfare?

— Peace is a political victory.

— That's what happened after the Troubles here, then, was it?

— It's not the same history. The contexts are different. It's hard to make comparisons. But, OK, you can if you like. So I guess you can see it as more or less the same thing.

— It's the same colonial history wherever you go.

— But here we had the famous handshake between Kanak and French and the country agreeing to take a chance on our common future.

— There are still some who refuse to take that step.

— One day their children will take it.

— Let's hope that everyone will share in this belief so that people finally stop killing one another in this life that's always over too soon and with no eternity waiting at the other end.

The powerful voice of Lucky Dube on Channel K reminds them of the singer's first concert in the country, where, well before they met, both of them had let themselves be carried away by his magical singing and its irresistible rhythms. Léna had gone on the first night with a group of girlfriends and not stopped dancing for the whole of the concert. Tom had gone too, with his own friends. And both of them had gone back again the second evening with the same groups to dance another night away to the beat of Lucky Dube's South African reggae.

They go on talking about the concert until they get to the village where, along with the passengers of several buses that were making a stop there, they both have a *café au lait* with *croissants* and *pain au chocolat*. One of Léna's friends appears and sits down with them. When Tom leaves the young women to go off and buy some bread, the friend takes advantage of his absence to tell Léna she is running away from a mother-in-law who is making her sick.

— Can she really do that? Léna asks her.

— Yes, she's been messing about with our 'business'.

— What do you mean, exactly?

— The old midnight brew, and stuff like that. You know, *le boucan*. Witchcraft.

— You can't let yourself believe in all that. It's not healthy.

— Maybe, but in the meantime she is, really.

— Hang on though, because if her plan is to try and separate you from her son, she'll be getting exactly what she's after if you go and run the hell away from her like this.

— Do you really think so? What should I do then?

— Go back home and stand up to her. Don't be afraid. Stand your ground and she'll end up leaving you alone.

— Thanks for the advice, Léna, I'll see what I can manage and let you know next time I see you. OK, bye, my bus is about to leave.

When the bus pulls out, Léna sees the old fisherman's face, staring at her out of the rear window. She can't contain a shiver but decides not to mention it to Tom so as not to spoil their journey.

They take their time driving slowly up the western side of the central mountain chain, to the rhythms of the *zouk*, the *salsa* and the *biguine*, mixed with the music of the Pacific. On the way down the other side, they take a side road toward a little clearing beside a creek in the forest. With a big towel draped around his neck, Tom helps Léna make her way through the moss and ferns of the undergrowth to the reeds that line the edge of the river flowing below them. Enchanted by the magic of the place, they make love on the stones beside the river, to the song of the water, in the first rays of sunshine. Then they go swimming and lie around, talking, playing and laughing. Tom pulls Léna back into the water and no longer meets any resistance. He is doubly certain that they have never loved each other as much as now, not even in the wreck, and that nothing will ever be able to separate them from this moment on. As they get ready to leave, Léna asks Tom, 'What did you say?'

— I didn't say a thing. What is it?

— I thought you were calling me.

— Now you're suffering from hallucinations and hearing voices, Tom joked. Tell me, my darling, you wouldn't happen to have been smoking a little *paka*,[28] would you?

— Shhh! Listen, someone's laughing up there. Can you hear?

— Yes, I can. Hunters maybe, coming along this path from the road.

— No, listen carefully. They're not coming from the road. It's someone laughing up there in the forest.

— Well, the hunters must be up there already, then.

Without saying any more, Léna simply walks back to the car in front of Tom. As they are not very familiar with the eastern side of the mountain chain, they again make it a slow, leisurely drive. They take the time to drink in the colours and sensations of the surrounding countryside, the forest, and the long river, as the road follows its slow, wending course. Then they find the sea, the coconut palms and little offshore islands. They stop for a snack on a small, isolated beach where a little creek, lost underground further upstream, re-emerges, bubbling up suddenly like a spring. As Léna spreads out their picnic mat, Tom is already running across the sand to dive into the transparent blue of the lagoon. Refusing to listen to what she once again hears as a voice calling her, she quickly joins Tom and they play in the waves like children

28 Cannabis (Transl.)

on holiday. Then he draws her down with him into the reeds and takes her lingeringly under the midday sun, once again meeting not the slightest resistance on her part.

They go back to rinse off the salt in the bubbles of the spring flowing out of the sand, then eat and lie down for a rest in the shade. Half-asleep on the mat, Léna starts awake when there crosses her field of vision the furtive outline of an old man, busy doing something or other over near a thicket of trees. She gets up and puts away their things, urging Tom to leave, barely hearing the greetings in their *paicî* language, the laughing *pwéélaa*[29] or 'how's things?' exchanged by young voices on Channel K.

When they reach the village of Léna's second mother, the other Léna – old Léna – comes out of her little round thatch house, from where the pungent odour of dried coconut leaves wafts up to meet them. Without showing the slightest sign of surprise, she invites them to sit around a table covered in a flowered plastic cloth, under the *tabou* tree, in a yard made fragrant by its flowers. Tom takes two lengths of fabric and two banknotes out of his bag and, in a voice charged with the emotion of this first meeting, and calling her 'mother', pronounces the words required to honour the ancestors of the place, the members of the clan and her, their elder relative. The lowered eyes of the two women indicate their own barely contained emotion. In an equally moved voice, old Léna then bids them welcome. As they had come into the village, Tom and Léna had planned to ask her where Tom's real mother lived, for they had never met her. When old Léna appeared at the door of her house, they both realised that, in fact, she was his mother. It's her. Léna's second mother is Tom's real mother. For all three, this long-awaited first meeting is immediately etched in their memory forever.

A meal of yams and fish cooked in coconut milk is followed by a cup of tea, while old Léna explains the order of ceremony for the wedding to take place that weekend. Then she leaves them to rest in the second bedroom of a neighbouring house, a rectangular building

29 In *cî* language meaning "how are you" or "how are things?" (Transl.)

with a corrugated iron roof and walls lined with particle board. She hurries down toward the beach and, weeping silently, makes her way straight to her usual place. There as she always does, she meets up with the man whose fishing ground it is.

— So, they've arrived, he says to her.

— Yes, and only God knows how long I've been waiting for them.

— Stop bringing God into it. It's like when you put on your best clothes to go and sing hymns of praise to Him on Sunday after you've been playing the whore all week here with me.

— Spare me your insults on the happiest day of my life!

— You don't spare me. You've never spared me. And you didn't spare her either. And nor have you spared the two of them. You're merciless.

— Be quiet.

— I don't set foot in God's house for I am not worthy and he alone knows my shame.

— Your shame, as you call it, has never stopped you from coming here just as you've come again today. And you have the nerve to call me a hypocrite and call me every name under the sun when I go and pray every Sunday.

— If it's not hypocrisy, then what is it, in your book?

— And when you come running here to find me, what is it? Only a dog doesn't hide to cover its mother.

— Well, I may be less than a dog but you're perfectly happy to get covered by me.

— Yes and you're always hanging around like a little poodle for its mistress to throw it a bone to gnaw on.

— You're the one who came back to the village while she was still alive, sniffing after me like some bitch in heat. You make me sick with what you did to her, especially when I look at those two kids. I don't want you anywhere near me. I'm leaving you to wallow in your own muck.

— That's what you've been saying all along, right from the start. But it does us both so much good feeling you inside me, I know you won't leave. Remember your wedding dinner when I was sitting opposite you both and you put your foot on my belly.

— And when I had another go that evening, you weren't wearing anything at all under your dress.

— And just after that while they were drinking, singing and dancing around the bride, you were on top of me, under the hedge behind the church where only that day you had sworn to be faithful to her.

— That's enough. Now I'm really leaving. You disgust me.

— And you were on me the night before your marriage, the morning and the night after, even while you were depositing children in her belly.

— Yes, I come back to you every time like a good little doggie, with my tail between my legs.

— And I'm always there on my knees, on all fours in front of you like a faithful old bitch waiting to get stuffed.

— You dirty old witch!

— Yes, that's it, the dirty old witch you come here everyday to fuck!

— Dirty old slut!

— Yes, the dirty old slut you come here everyday to hump!

— Dirty old bitch!

— Yes, the dirty old bitch you come here everyday to mount!

— I'm gonna fuck you to death.

— Yes, yes that's it. Come on Daddy-O! Come till you die in the old hole of your old grandmother bitch.

— Oh Yes! I'm gonna give that old bitch-on-heat hole of yours what's coming to it, grandma, he moaned, leaning into her toothless open mouth, across which a stray lock of white hair had fallen.

Jumping back to his feet, he runs off to lie in the spring, bubbling up out of the sand on the neighbouring beach, as if to cleanse himself. Then, as he goes off, with his net over his shoulder along the beaten earth track to join the elders of the clan around the lengths of cloth, banknotes, clothes and *âdi*[30] for the marriage ceremony, she too goes over to the sandy spring. She lets her body, softened by love-making, slide down into the water. Softly humming a local tune, she wallows in the water and the sand, drinking it all in and smiling to herself as she remembers their first rendezvous.

It was a long time ago, the time when Éva was being drawn into the religious sect; one Friday morning, at the central bus station. He had just arrived from the *tribu* by bus and she had invited him for a coffee, and then to lunch, and after to the movies where they were showing The Graduate with Simon and Garfunkel's Mrs Robinson. Everything about him seemed familiar and she went back to Éva's and slept with him in the hut that had been reserved for the men in a happier early time when they were young and loved to party. It was the time of love. Love affairs were born, enjoyed, cooled, and died as quickly as desires; needs and feelings changed. Love then was heedless of time, morality, and custom. It was the time of free love. Twosomes, threesomes, or more – with men, women, either or both, in the drunkenness of liquor and the night of the senses. 'To make life' as the old people used to call it.

Léna felt a sense of lingering nostalgia for this period. The hut no longer offered hospitality to any except close relatives. Less and less, in fact, as Éva let herself be drawn into a religious sect where a combination of brainwashing and Bible-bashing rendered her increasingly like Molière's punishing statue of the commander in his moralising version of Don Juan. Every day, she became more and more of a pillar of Christian morality that no one dared challenge for fear of being burned up in all the fires of hell and damnation. Mistaking herself for the biblical Eve of paradise lost, she now saw in every man, a possible incarnation of the seductive serpent ready to squeeze you to death in his coils like a boa constrictor. And, in Léna – who was totally nonplussed by this unexpected enthusiasm for a sect Éva had hitherto abhorred – she thought she saw a kind of double of herself, mired in sin. Amongst other objectives, she set herself the task of dragging Léna up out of the

30 Length of shells pearls, shells, flying-fox bone, and fern, a symbol of the person in customary exchanges (Transl.).

muck and this gave rise to interminable daily sermons on the fate of the adulterous or fallen woman. Léna, who remained quite astounded by all this, would say to her with a smile:

— But Maria, I've never had a husband. I'm no Mary Magadalene either. And you shouldn't mistake yourself for the Holy Virgin, the mother of *Jésu Kériso*.[31]

— You're blaspheming, blaspheming child of the devil! Don't you dare pronounce the name of the Holy Virgin or *Jésu Kéri*so while you're still bedding in the muck of sin!

— But Éva, it wasn't so very long ago, you too were wallowing around in the mud of the garden and the mangroves with Madame and me.

— Precisely. That's why I don't go to the garden anymore. Or crab-fishing in the mangroves.

— Why? Afraid of getting your hands dirty now? That the kind of idea those new friends of yours have been putting into your head?

— They haven't been putting any ideas into my head. I listened to them and chose to follow the path of the word of God. That's all.

— Coming from someone like you, who used to be a kind of mother figure for all of us, passing on the old customary ways and all that, let's just say we all find your ninety-degree turn to religion rather kind of hard to swallow!

— Those days are well and truly over. And now you're going to get out of here the lot of you because what counts most for me now is God. I don't want to live in sin any more and burn in hell when I die.

— But Éva, you're the one who taught me that death returned us to the earth, our eternal resting place.

— Get behind me, *Sâtanâ*![32] Beware, judgement day is nigh!

— Éva, Listen to me! Oh Éva, whatever have they done to you?

This was the kind of debate that would flare up between the two women at frequent intervals at about the time when Léna brought the young man back to their place. One fine morning, he followed her

---

31 Jesus Christ in several Kanak languages. (Transl.)
32 Satan in *cî* language. (Transl.)

to the mangroves where she pulled him down into the thicket that had harboured her earlier, female, love affairs and the two of them began a forbidden and doomed passion, in defiance of customary law. And Éva, who had decided to put them under her righteous surveillance, following the example of Madame, whose binoculars she had borrowed for the occasion, had found them there. When they returned, she had already thrown their belongings out of the house. She then proceeded to rebuke them:

— I thought customary law made it unlawful for you two to fornicate!

— Custom or your sect, Éva? Léna retorted.

— You owe me respect, after everything I've given you in this house, you worthless little hussy!

— And you've taken it all back to go and bury yourself in your damned sect. Besides, it was out of respect for you, the two of us didn't do anything under your roof.

— God sees everything you do, daughter of the devil! You get yourself pregnant to that old pimp of a fisherman, and you give your name to his daughter with Maria. Yes, because I know that whenever you two were at a loose end you went back with her to see Old Tom who gave you to his whole gang over at the wreck. You were his two favourite whores in that wreck. It banged around in all directions when he used to hump the both of you in there, that dirty, filthy old dog. You pushed Maria into the arms of the first sucker who came along, to give little Léna a father. Just like you did to find a mother for your son, Tom, up there in the *tribu*. Take it from me, you are the daughter of *Sâtanâ*. And now, you're getting yourself laid by your little brother, who's also the son that old sorcerer gave your aunt, before he went running off with you, his own daughter! So, you truly are the daughter of the devil, because that's just who that cursed old sorcerer is! He's the devil in person! Do you dare deny it.

— Hang on a bit, Éva. You were also with Old Tom, well before us. So what exactly are you trying to say, here?

Oh really? So now you're going to try and tell me it's not true? You liar.

All your sins will be visited upon you and upon your children. It's written in the Bible. Get out of my house, now – out with the both of you!

— Wait, Éva. Just one last thing!

— Wait Éva, wait for what? Once upon a time, I spent all my time waiting for you. And now I need to do the work of God, I've got no more time to waste. Not on a worthless hussy like you. What are you waiting for? What do you want now?

— Well Éva, doesn't forgiveness exist in your sect?

— There's no forgiveness for black sheep.

— Yes, but doesn't your Good Shepherd love his whole flock? Éva don't you feel any pity for me? You used to. Read us the passage about the woman taken in adultery that you used to like so much.

At the end of the reading, Léna asked her gently, one last time,

— So you're going to cast the first stone at me now?

— Go, woman and sin no more, murmured Éva from the doorway before closing the door in the couple's face and collapsing onto her bed.

Léna whispered to her companion,

— If Éva thinks she's *Jésu Kériso*, then you and I are Adam and Eve.

So Léna left her for good to follow the young man from the *tribu*, even though, by customary law, their kinship forbade the relationship. They hung around for a while with friends in the city who either didn't know about it or turned a blind eye. Léna was reliving, without too many qualms, the situation she had experienced earlier with the fisherman. They finally separated, at least officially, to save appearances, pressured by members of the clan who took the young man back to the *tribu* to marry him off. But he looked her up whenever he was in town, especially in the wreck, where the night sheltered their lovemaking after nights of partying that sometimes brought them back to the old fisherman's place. In the end, she too returned to the *tribu* where their affair began again, even more passionately. Some of the other women, female relatives from the same clan, insulted her and attacked her, beating her violently. The wife died during the birth of her third child. Ostracised, then assaulted several times by the same women, Léna found herself in the hospital in town, where her lover rushed to her bedside. It was there that she learned that Éva, cheated out of her tithes by one of the pastors of the sect who had made her his mistress, had lost her reason and had to be committed. One Saturday afternoon as she gazed out toward the wreck, her mind went back to the time of her affair with Maria and the fisherman. He then turned up in the evening to say that her young lover had been at his house since the previous evening and was cooking up a nice little meal that would no doubt be accompanied with plenty of good wine to celebrate her birthday. When he offered to take her there, she followed him without asking any questions. This was also a way of getting away from the prison-like environment and medicinal odours she loathed at the hospital and, even more so, from the patronising and cloying sweetness of the nurses, who spoke down to their patients as if they were children. In the wreck, that evening, her lover made her forget all the wounds of her being. Soon after, he went back to the *tribu* – and it wasn't long before she followed. Once there, they agreed not to meet from then on, except down in the bush by the sanctuary of the black rock, the wreck of the great canoe.

After a cup of tea under the *tabou* tree, the old woman takes Tom and Léna to the meal farewelling the future bride. As she had been asked to, she presents the couple's share of lengths of fabric, dresses, banknotes and boxes of food to the customary authorities of the clan. One of them, none other than her lover of the sanctuary, thanks them for their gifts with great eloquence, offering a length of *manou*[33] cloth in return and stressing the need for future generations to maintain these traditional forms of solidarity. His oratory is clear and fluent and he speaks with the confidence of those whose traditional role is to be the bearer of the Word of their clan. He charms his audience, seducing them with such natural ease that the stories circulating about his suspect goings-on simply vanish from people's minds. In particular, the one that goes back the furthest and is the most dubious.

33   Piece of cloth with oceanian motifs – like a *paréo* (Transl.)

But his grandfather had told him so many times that the Word, gift of the gods and invisible breath of the ancestors had nothing to do with what went on in the grass, in the hay, or in the bushes; that he clearly saw no connection between the two. The shame, disgust and repulsion that he speaks of to his aging lover are merely part of a game of mutual arousal, the goal of which is that fleeting pleasure of the senses that liberates the body from what might otherwise hinder the flow of the Word. And she, for her part, was so good at that game of bringing them both to ecstasy that he had never wanted, nor been able, to give her up. In comparison with this force of attraction for both of them, their kinship relation was merely an unfortunate accident and, in any event, completely beyond their control, theirs or anyone else's. Although everyone in the *tribu* knew about them, as long as they kept up appearances by only seeing each other in secret, the pact that binds the community remained intact. Besides which, no one really wants to destroy that bond, or disturb the order of things; with the result that even the most virulent of the women had ended up more or less putting up with them.

And so every man and every woman takes his and her designated place at the dinner to farewell the future bride, while the younger ones serve the meal. The time reserved for speech-making allows them to thank one another, recall customary links, offer prayers and announce the coming sequence of events in the marriage programme scheduled for the following day. This provides the orator with a further opportunity to capture the attention of all those present with his mastery of the art and the power invested in him as the master of the Word. Every time he does so, she lowers her head like the others as a sign of respect. She knows that he is taking on the social role handed down through generation upon generation to those of his gender, his clan and his rank. Unlike others, he has not chosen to shirk these responsibilities to go off and live with her somewhere else. He has chosen to live out his role within the clan, fitting her into his life as far as possible. In other words, on the side. Thus, she had accepted, earlier on, his customary marriage that was part and parcel of this choice.

For this reason, she had put up with the beatings, shouldered the blame, taken the entire fault upon herself, so as to allow him to exercise the rights and duties he owed their people. She had chosen to continue to give herself to him in the shadows, rather than leave. That would only have pushed him into running off after her, abandoning the responsibilities his grandfather had educated him for. She knew that she would always be bottom of the list but she didn't care. It was nothing compared to the love and the voluptuous pleasure of their shared moments. She's still got that. What he can't give her, she can live without. The violence of the insults they hurl at one another is an integral part of the game of passion that binds them, within the circle of taboo and in defiance of it. This violence is an expression of the carnal reality of naked desire, of senses excited by the inexorable fascination of breaking social codes dressed up as inviolable law.

At the table, the guests' mouths water at the gargantuan selection of food and drinks laid out before them: A whole array of salads, fish, seafood, meats, cordials, wines and desserts. Green salads, Russian salads, Tahitian salads, asparagus rolls wrapped in ham, curried eggs, shredded crab-meat and crayfish, carrot salad, choko salad, coleslaws of white and red cabbage. The spread of roast meats boasts fine slices of beef, venison, deer, pork and chicken. There are fried food platters, of tuna, sardines, picot, *becs de canne*,[34] sausages, bananas, kumara and potatoes. Skewers of barbecued meat sit alongside *notou* pigeon in sauce, and platters of well-fattened *roussette* on beds of *ambrevade* peas.[35] Dishes of white rice sit next to Cantonese fried rice, Vietnamese *bami* and spring rolls. There are cooked bananas and roasted manioc root, white yams and purple yams and every variety of kumara – orange, yellow, violet and cream. Mullet in coconut milk compete with pungent *dawas*, whose bursting skins reveal an oily flesh. There are pumpkin and choko hearts, Kanak greens and sticky cabbage. The flower-decorated *bougna* parcels from the earth oven open to reveal chicken, *roussette*, and fish topped with fresh herbs.

---

34 *Lethrinus*. (Transl.)

35 Pigeon Pea, *Cajanus cajan*. (Transl.)

Green parcels of taro leaves, bananas and grated manioc complement dishes of roasted eel, pork, meats and smoked fish served on delicate plates woven from young coconut fronds.

Jugs of sparkling clear water and of grenadine – red, lemon yellow, mint green and orange cordials, their colours evoking their flavour – stand tall among bottles of red, rosé and white wine – from aperitifs to dry whites, and sparkling wines, from calvados to champagne, from burgundy to bordeaux and côtes-du-rhône. Table wines preside over spirits, apéritifs and digestifs, labelled muscat, martini, vodka, whisky, cognac, or cointreau. Sugar-coloured plastic bottles and cans of fruit juice and soda, beers, shandies and liqueurs are lined up next to bottles of condiments – salt and pepper, soy sauce and *Maggi* sauce. Desserts will be offered, when the time comes, to round off the feast – gateaux oozing with cream, fruit tarts, vanilla, chocolate and banana ice cream and tropical fruit salads.

The orator seats himself opposite Léna, between Tom and his own eldest son, also the eldest son of the clan according to custom, and whose wife is about to give birth at the local clinic. As she sips her aperitif, Léna smiles at him, feeling his sharp, penetrating gaze probing the base of her throat. Throughout the entrée and the salad, he eats, talks and jokes, without taking his admiring flirtatious eyes off her. He hands her the main courses with a seductive smile, lightly brushing her fingers. When he serves her the wine, she thanks him, letting the tip of her tongue flick over the rim of her glass of rosé. Devouring a spring roll, he holds her gaze as he gently slides the palm of his hand over the rounded belly of a water jug. Biting into a sausage, she stretches out her hand towards a bottle of wine that he is quick to pick up, favouring her with a surreptitious caress as he does so, before serving her. When the *bougnas* are brought out, she feels his bare foot on her own, then the end of his toes between her knees. He talks to Tom while keeping his hot, unblinking gaze firmly on her, turning the end of his index finger around and around inside the neck of a soda-bottle. She pushes herself a little further toward the edge of her seat to provide easier access for his big toe, which slips under the hem of her dress and begins to explore her methodically. The young woman's entire body starts to burn at this unexpected contact that rivets her to this man, under the table, unbeknownst to all. He raises his glass with his eyes fixed on her, inviting her to do the same, and takes a long swig. Her belly on fire beneath his predatory toe, she complies, replying 'yes, yes' when he asks 'is it good?', running her tongue over her lips, just as he had. Feeling her catch fire, shaking with silent spasms, he can read her orgasm from her half-opened mouth and misty gaze.

He bends forward, reaching down under the table as if to scratch his toe. Straightening up and grinning broadly, his gaze holding that of the young woman, he passes his index finger under his nostrils, then along the tip of his tongue.

Léna recovers herself as the voices of the *tapéras* singers ring out, honouring the guests with their hymns and drowning out the general hubbub. Their voices fill the long flower-covered shelter with its roof of corrugated iron and walls of woven green palm leaves, constructed especially for the wedding.

During dessert, he tells an old local story where a very young fisherman steps on a small clam by mistake and it closes shut on his big toe. It hurts a lot, but the flesh of the shellfish helps take away the pain. Unable to separate himself from the shellfish, he lives with it, taking it back to the sea everyday when he goes fishing. The smell of the sea encourages the shell to open up but it also likes the taste of the toe that feeds it. However, the call of the sea is stronger and the clamshell finally opens on the big toe that by this time it had eaten up entirely. The fisherman no longer suffers from the wound that has healed over. He picks up the clam intending to cook it and eat it. He does a little more fishing in the area, but he no longer has his big toe to catch clams with. And that is why you can always recognise his tracks on the sand.

Léna knows that the story is for her alone, sealing the unseen capture of her body under the table by the storyteller. She knows already that later, during the night, he will again make her his thing, his object, his slave, as and when he pleases. She doesn't worry about Tom, who the storyteller has evidently been working on getting drunk since the beginning of the meal, laughing uproariously with the future husband. Indeed, late in the evening, he takes her furiously against the trunk of a coconut palm. Their mutual pleasure is heightened by the sight of a drunken Tom, deep in conversation with his mother, old Léna. Their bodies perfectly physically attuned, they go back to the area set up for dancing. Completely absorbed by their new union, amidst the densely packed crowd of dancers, they don't even hear Tom call out joyously, raising his glass and telling them that the grandson of the orator, born at dawn will also be called Tom, at old Léna's suggestion to the happy father. Later still, and barely able to stand on his feet, he asks them to drive him home. He collapses on the back seat while they get into the front where the orator can caress Léna at will, all the way home. They help Tom get into bed then make love in a variety of positions on the earth floor, in earshot of his snoring. When Léna falls asleep against Tom, exhausted, the orator slips into the next bedroom to wait for his old lover. When she arrives, somewhat under the influence, he makes her get down on her knees in front of him and tells her the detail of everything he has done to her young namesake since the meal. The proximity of the sleeping young couple stimulates senses aroused by the events of the day and the evening celebrations. Taking her by her white hair, he pulls her hard up against him and enters her mouth, ordering her to cleanse him of anything that might remain from the belly of the other.

In the morning, he is already there having coffee with the elders of the clan when they turn up, before they sit down together to share out the work of the Word. As the one who is to give away the woman, he must remind them, first of all, of the links forged by the marriage alliance, then of the function and the role of women. Then he must ask forgiveness for her, in the event she unwittingly transgresses any taboo. Then, following the program laid out together by the clans of the bridal couple, the women prepare the young girl to bear her large bridal basket of woven green coconut leaves full of taro. As she comes out of the thatch house, her basket on her back, they surround her, singing the song for the departure of the bride in the local language. The words praise the beauty of her expression, her fine complexion and graceful body, and urge her to stand and go forth to a very beautiful new land. They also speak her farewell to her people who will have to visit her in her new land. The orator and the men come toward them as the procession advances amidst general good humour, singing, joking, laughing and calling. The two Lénas walk forward, arms around each other's waist, their eyes fixed on the lover they now share since the previous night. He jokes with them, rumpling the bright-coloured silken fabric of their dresses as he clasps first one and then the other around the hips, kneading the flesh with his hands. Tom photographs them like this, a new love trio, offering themselves to the camera and laughing irrepressibly. Old Léna knows that, from this moment, she will get every bit as much as pleasure as her lover from the young body they are progressively taking in their possession.

Songs welcome the clan of the bride and its allies, and continue while the mats are unrolled and the lengths of fabric, dresses, shirts, trousers and *âdi*, the traditional 'money', are laid out in two parts for the customary exchange. The orator greets them first of all with lengths of cloth wrapped around an *âdi*, reminding them of the ancient links uniting lineages and fraternal clans. He speaks of the enduring importance of solidarity, particularly necessary in periods of mourning and to obtain the blessing of the ancestors required for the proper performance of work in the shade of their pines and coconut palms. He finishes to the general applause of his audience.

Then he sits down beside the bride with her basket and three of her closest relatives. Taking other lengths of material and passing their brightly coloured folds between his thumb and index fingers, barely managing to contain the emotion in his voice, he calls out, two by two, in the local oratorical tradition, the names of all the visiting clans whose representatives he sees before him. Voices are raised to urge him on, others signal their approval by repeating loudly the traditional formula, *üü*.[36] He goes through the same exercise for the group of local clans for whom he is the spokesperson, and who are there to accompany the young girl they have raised and educated. Using the traditional symbols of fire and the cooking-pot, he proclaims the vital role of woman in the life and the relationships between clans. As a mother, she provides food and guarantees the transmission of life from generation to generation. As a sister and a wife, she is, through marriage, the pathway of alliance between the clans. The audience grows louder and more encouraging with every mention.

The orator stands before the second share of gifts, with a third roll of fabric, and asks the relatives of the groom to pardon the young bride in advance, for broken dishes or for the involuntary breaking of taboos, in particular those taboos linked to the earth. The speech ends with a final round of general applause.

After the men have rolled up the contents of the two shares of gifts offered by the guests and put them away, the orator for the husband's side calls them to take tea or coffee under the long flower-covered shelter. While one group goes inside, others stay outside and start singing. Léna lets herself be carried away by the collective joy animating the whole *tribu* close beside her old *deviné*, her namesake and her 'double'. Likewise, Tom sticks by the son of the orator, as if he were a long-forgotten brother. Léna's whole being now hangs on the decision of the man who had taken possession of her so utterly during the farewell meal the evening before. The glances they exchange remind each other of this situation as they watch for an opportunity to be alone. Unable to hold out any longer, he goes up to her, still singing, and tells her to go and wait for him at his house. And Léna slips between the singers and runs to his house without a murmur.

---

36 "Yes", in the *cî* language, uttered by an audience, during a speech, to show approval. The tone changes according to the genre: speech, story, poem. (Transl.)

The ancestor on the *flèche faîtière*, the roof-spire adorned with conch shells, watches her coming through the pines, like a woman alone in a canoe on the high seas breaking through the waves of passion. Like tropical sirens, the birds offer her their deceptive songs. She brushes against the *cordylines*, the customary gift for the newborn used to obtain the 'breath of life' from the accepting maternal uncles. Just sensing her nearness is enough to take away the unfaithful breath of the lover already waiting inside, as finally, she slips between the two ancient guardians of the door who fix her with their wooden stare. He welcomes her with a burning kiss that consumes her entirely in the half-light. This brief and intense embrace, in full daylight, in his house, on another's wedding-day, is also a declaration. It means his speeches were intended for her too, that from now on he considers her to be his wife, that she must stay with him, at his disposal, in the *tribu*, and not go back to town. He gets up, telling her to close her flesh tight shut around him and never let him go, like the clam in the story. He hears her 'yes' of submission several times as, naked at his feet, she writhes around beneath his big toe which explores deep inside her. As for old Léna, she is wriggling around in the same position, in the neighbouring coffee plantation, with a young lover she has just picked up. Having observed the couple sneaking away separately from the wedding celebrations, she just had to have a partner to help her live out her fantasies of what those two might be up to.

When they return, the *porte-parole* of the bride's clan, as master of ceremonies, calls them, firstly to present and then to return, everything that has been offered to them in the customary ceremonial exchange. After this, the bride and groom put on their wedding attire; fancy suit and tie for the groom and white mission dress for the bride. They sit down in front of the mayor with their retinue: Best man, bridesmaids, little maids of honour in their doll's dresses, grooms of honour in bowties, and all the extended family, at the flower-decked table of the local town hall. After replying 'yes' to the questions traditionally asked at French civil weddings, the mayor gives them their *livret de famille*; their official family record book. Then the procession makes its way to the Protestant church on a little hill opposite, where it is the pastor's turn to bless their union, between the singing of hymns and readings of biblical verses on marital love and the total submission of the woman to the man.

The orator's gaze meets Léna's and she lowers her eyes to see his big toe moving under the leather of his sandal as he intones the next hymn. Old Léna, who can see everything, laughs silently to herself at this secret code which she had originated by telling him the story of the fisherman and the clam in the thicket at the edge of the mangroves, on the morning of their first sexual encounter. She had learnt it from the old fisherman who often took pleasure playing the big toe under the table with her during their evenings of wild sex, over there by the wreck, just as Éva did too, at the time when she was keeping open-house at her place. She had also invented the other big toe game, the one that involved squirming around on the ground in naked submission. Thinking about it, she can hardly stop herself bursting into hysterical laughter and is relieved to hear the last amen of the religious ceremony.

The hymn-singing begins again in front of the long shelter decked with flowers for the wedding. A little inebriated, some of the *tapéras* singers begin to raise the volume as tenor, alto and soprano all compete to make themselves heard. Little by little, the choir drowns out the noise of conversations, the jokes and cries and the laughter of children competing to outrun and outplay one another. Then the spokesman for the husband's clan invites people to file in behind the couple who are seated in the place of honour. When the two long tables constructed for the occasion are full, the pastor blesses the meal, before the singers on the husband's side begin intoning *tapéras* again.

The meal begins with the aperitif and the cordials. The children raise their multicoloured plastic glasses of fizzy drink. Except for those who are teetotallers or on special diets, after the toast to the bridal couple, every one has his glass of champagne or whisky, gin, or punch. Plates of nibbles are passed around before the entrées and the salads. Then come the main dishes, the *bougnas*, cuts of pork, yams, taros, sweet potatoes, manioc and roast pumpkin. Red wine follows white wine and rosé. The orator takes turns with his big toe under the table with both Lénas, who accept his attentions as their due. The meal is coming to an end when the women dance in, one after the other, some carrying the wedding cake, others holding out the long lengths of cloth. They put the French *pièce montée*[37] down in front of the wedding couple who stand up to cut it, their hands together on the knife, while champagne corks pop. Slices of cake and tall glasses of bubbly are passed around to the tune of wedding songs.

After the meal, the couple sit on a bench with their witnesses to receive their presents. The procession of relatives and friends begins to the sound of *tapéras*. Parcels, banknotes, lengths of fabric – each one places their gift in a special cardboard box. At dusk, they are counted and the total value announced. After the evening meal, there are different festivities – a ball, a customary *pilou*, and a choir singing *tapéras*, so the crowd separates off into groups. Old Léna, aware that her namesake is going to go off with the orator, lets the two of them go off first. To avoid any unpleasant surprises for Tom, the lover makes sure he returns to the wedding a little later. Léna is exhausted by the long day of celebration and lovemaking. Later again, while she is dozing peacefully beside Tom, sleeping off his wine, in the neighbouring room, the orator and old Léna resume their habitual pleasures.

The following day, towards the end of the afternoon, after sharing out the customary gifts given by the clan of the husband and his extended family to their new allies, Tom gets ready to go back to town without Léna, who says she has a very bad headache. In an early morning nightmare, she had heard the sardonic, laughing voice of the old fisherman. She had seen his grin and his strange gnome-like body as he pointed insistently toward the bottom of a deep ravine where a canoe lay, tossing on a stormy sea.

— The wreck's down there.

---

37 Pyramid of small, round custard-filled choux buns held together with caramel. (transl. note.)

These images seem to be bad omens to her and she warns Tom against getting behind the wheel late on Sunday evening with a hangover. He tries to reassure her, singing along to Bob Marley on the radio as he starts the car: 'So, don't worry, *chérie*, listen to Bob and wait for me, I'll be back on Saturday. Come on. Don't look so upset. You remind me of my little cuz, your ex, when I woke up from a nightmare like this one on the morning we met. And look, I'm still here, right here in front of you! Hey! Come on babe, *No woman no cry*, as Bob says! I love you. See you on Saturday!'

Tom will not return on Saturday. He will fall asleep as he takes a corner, not see his car slip into the ravine of Léna's nightmare, the same visions and the same words of the old fisherman running through his weary head. His younger cousin will read about it on the front-page news – how they found a little black rosette with a red heart (from the wedding celebrations) lying on the grass near the wreck of the vehicle, as if someone had placed it there. Further on, another article relates that, following the crime of the bay, the old fisherman answering to the name of Tom the tramp, well known around those parts, had been arrested after being dobbed in by an anonymous witness. The witness said he had seen him, that very morning, assaulting Lila, who was believed to have run away from her father's house in a mining centre, to follow him.

A prisoner of her senses, of her body, with all her being totally under the control of the old couple, the orator and her namesake, Léna will have three children, one of whom will also be called Léna, at the insistence of old Léna. Little by little, she will come to feel an intense hatred toward the pair because of the power they wield over her. And one day, when the orator pulls her into the clump of bushes down by the canoe cemetery, she will recognise the black rock where someone raped her in her early childhood, during a picnic with her parents, Léna, her second mother, and two others. One of the two was a lot younger, an adolescent.

She observes him now, the orator, walking in front of her at the edge of the cliff looking over the shark hole, a spot sometimes indeed infested by sharks. He makes a false move and slips, grabbing hold of

162

the edge of a rock. He begs her to pull him up. For the first time, she reads supplication in his face. For the first time, she sees tears in his eyes. And she recognises him.

The veil across the depths of her memory is suddenly torn aside. She sees once again the scene of the rape of her young child's body by the orator, an adolescent at the time, under the complicit watching eye of the fisherman, he too, using and abusing her like a doll on the black rock of the wreck.

Léna forgets about the sharks swimming around below and runs off to the sound of something heavy falling into the water behind her. She comes face to face with her namesake who calls out to her accusingly, 'Where is he? Where is he?' She points to the sea below the cliff and old Léna runs towards it, her heart beating as it does at every one of their rendezvous. Léna turns round just in time to see her jump and hear her scream die away in the waves.

On the beach, she finds the two children, Tom and Léna, who came down with their grandmother. Little Tom, the grandson of the orator and her own little Léna. They will come here often with the others. And one afternoon, when they are adolescents, they will take an age to answer her calls. They will take forever to return from the grove of the wreck of the great canoe. Where, there on the black stone, they are learning to love.